TIGHT SHIPS DON'T SINK

PROFIT SECRETS FROM A NO-NONSENSE CEO

GARY SUTTON with Brian Tarcy

PRENTICE HALL
Englewood Cliffs, New Jersey 07632

Prentice-Hall International (UK) Limited, *London*
Prentice-Hall of Australia Pty. Limited, *Sydney*
Prentice-Hall Canada, Inc., *Toronto*
Prentice-Hall Hispanoamericana, S.A., *Mexico*
Prentice-Hall of India Private Limited, *New Delhi*
Prentice-Hall of Japan, Inc., *Tokyo*
Simon & Schuster Asia Pte. Ltd., *Singapore*
Editora Prentice-Hall do Brasil, Ltda., *Rio de Janeiro*

10 9 8 7 6 5 4 3 2 1

Library of Congress Cataloging-in-Publication Data

Sutton, Gary.
Tight ships don't sink : profit secrets from a no-nonsense CEO by Gary Sutton with Brian Tarcy.
p. cm.
Includes index.
ISBN 0-13-035973-4
1. Small business—Management. 2. Small business—Management—Cost control. I. Tarcy, Brian. II. Title.
HD62.7.S98 1993
658.02'2—dc20 93-4454
CIP

ISBN 0-13-035973-4

Printed in the United States of America

A Few Words About *Tight Ships Don't Sink . . .*

"A solid guide from one who's been there." Peter Ueberroth

"Finally! How-to-profit." John Carrington, CEO, Digitalk

"Hard-hitting, practical thrusts." Philip Thurston, Professor Emeritus, Harvard Graduate School of Business

"Uncommon, in-your-face, killer thinking." Carole Rhoades, Vice-President, Seaport Ventures

"Powerful. I re-read on trips." Allan Shaw, Executive Director, MS Society

"Executives must get this." Martha J. Demski, Vice President & CFO, Fical

"Winning basics for sports, war or business." Don Drobny, Partner, Perot Systems

to Nancy, my rudder

ACKNOWLEDGMENTS

Michael Snell, a perceptive literary agent, talked with and studied me late in 1992. Snell noted that there hadn't been a hands-on management book since *Up the Organization* swept the country two decades ago. He suggested this title and format and almost promised that a publisher would buy it if I could merely outline *Tight Ships Don't Sink*. Then he introduced Brian Tarcy.

Tarcy, rock-and-rolling former columnist and Cleveland Indians fan, sprinkled color over my drab verbiage, making these chapters readable to you. He cut the fat, told me when more was needed and kept the stories on track. And more than once he explained that a particular concept was a yawn, so you were not burdened with those chapters.

Tom Power, senior editor at Prentice Hall, was one of several publishers expressing interest. But Power sent the first advance check, clinching the deal. More important, he gently counseled Tarcy and me afterwards, as we wrote, with small touches that were big enhancements. Now I know why he enjoys universal respect in the publishing industry.

There's a large crew of co-workers, customers, competitors, vendors, and owners who inspired these tactics and stories. Most are noted on these pages. A couple of names and places were disguised to save embarrassment.

Thank you each for making this book so easy to write.

By the way, it all works. Tight ships don't sink.

INTRODUCTION

They found the *Titanic,* now a grave. Bob Ballard led the dive to find the old boat that was first a dream, then glitzy reality and quickly a tragedy. The *Titanic.* An omen for business in the '90s—all flash, all lying under 12,000 feet of icy salt water.

Ballard did what no one else could. He found the unsinkable ship. Ballard found it because he did what the makers and captain of the "unsinkable" *Titanic* didn't. He ran a tight ship.

1,513 passengers drowned in the North Atlantic that black night. This group was smaller than the smallest of recent IBM, General Motors, or Sears layoffs. The *Titanic* was extraordinary. Its image is eerily familiar in business.

Corporate *Titanics* are everywhere. Sears, General Motors, and IBM all suck seawater today. Their captains rearrange deck chairs, throw crew overboard, and blast foghorns at approaching rocks. Small companies sink so fast they don't even leave an oil slick.

This needn't be. I know. In the last two decades, I've been a principal and officer of both a telecom business and a toy manufacturer. They began as startups and within years billion dollar outfits acquired each. Neither operated like a *Titanic.* Both had the system, a simple set of rules everybody followed.

This system evolved from many years in many businesses. It flexes to fit the situation but stays steady in attitude. Discipline works.

I learned long ago, working for Lennox Industries, that discipline does not mean stifling creativity. Quite the contrary. Discipline opens up creative thinking.

When that is understood, all else falls into place.

Discipline is the framework of any business ship. It applies everwhere, from choosing what kind of company to be, to raising organizational ethics. All the while riding a big wave of profits. This is not theory. This is not philosophy.

This is how.

I decided to write *Tight Ships Don't Sink* when, because of my luck with a few startups and turnarounds, people asked if I had developed some secret formula. Yup. I've got the formula.

As CEO, I put together the largest commercial printing group in the west. I salvaged and sold a PC supplies distributor and an aerospace manufacturer. Right now I run a burglar alarm company. These companies ranged from a thousand employees to thirty. Most were private but some were public. The same simple techniques always worked. And the happy investors became wealthier during my tenure.

In time, and unplanned, I became a turnaround guy. The formula is so simple it's embarrassing. And if you're the CEO of a troubled business, let's hope we never meet. When I arrive, you leave. But the whole idea of *Tight Ships Don't Sink* is to show how we all avoid that unpleasantness. Run a tight ship and you'll never see me.

This book tells how.

I offer here fifty-one business stories. Some tragic, some victorious, all real world just as the *Titanic* was once. The *Titanic* is the ideal business example for our age.

There were gold chandeliers, fine bone china, and great staterooms but not enough lifeboats. There was majestic size (the largest ship then built) a self-conscious luxury and an aura of invincibility. But the hull ripped like cheap cloth.

When Bob Ballard went looking for the *Titanic,* he didn't go with glitz. He went with function and he didn't skip any steps. That's how to run a tight ship. That's how to run a business. Work hard, think wide-open, and always trim costs. It pays off. Tight Ships Don't Sink.

Following each of these fifty-one real-world stories are three action steps to improve profitability. Every last one of these 153 profit-boosting tactics works. You'll see how to:

—hire smarter
—neuter unions
—make ethics pay
—banish sex, drugs, and God
—eliminate firing fear
—tame the computer
—slash legal expense
—capture minority productivity
—spot new product winners
—stop educational discrimination

plus one hundred more outrageous, proven tactics. Use them and your business will miss all the icebergs.

And yes, profits shall multiply.

CONTENTS

PART 1

COMPASS READINGS: Charting a Straight Business Path

CHAPTER 1

Raise a Flag

The store manager was stunned by the numbers. His chain, Home Depot, knew all about rapid success, but this printout was staggering. He had found a way to add $14 million a year in profitable sales with no risk or investment. Fourteen million dollars!

He tapped his pencil on his desk. He picked up a pen and drumrolled the two together. And then he pushed his chair back from his desk and clasped his hands behind his head with the confidence of a corporate hero.

He sprang from his chair and bounced to the door. He thought about how much fun it was to say the words "million dollars" and so he said them fourteen times. He opened the door and before him lay his Home Depot, a link in the 160-unit chain, going to 522 by 1997. At the time, sales were approaching $5 billion a year. And he was contributing. Nothing minor either: a $14 million discovery.

He walked from his office through his Home Depot feeling like a bright merchant prince in an orange apron. He knew it well. Sure, he learned some from training, but mostly he learned by doing. He kept walking, strolling. He surveyed the screen doors, mirrors, drills, sinks, shower heads, drapes, toilets, garden fencing, tools, light fixtures, rugs, sprinkling systems, paintbrushes, saws, mattresses, lawn mowers, beds, and garbage cans. He knew where every item belonged, and he knew most prices. This was his turf.

He looked at it and he looked past it, ambling toward something at the front of the store. All the while there was confidence, a gait to his walk.

Three months earlier, this manager had agreed to put a small kiosk near the cash registers. It was a simple test. The kiosk held one thing: Hanes hosiery for women. The Hanes distributor would keep it stocked and the Home Depot would pay in 60 days. The nylons sold for $3 a pair, and Home Depot was invoiced for $2.40 each. The kiosk took up only four of the 102,000 square feet of his store.

IT HAD BEEN five years since the first Home Depot opened in Atlanta. The idea was to sell everything for the home. With a 102,000-square-foot store, there was a selection much broader than the typical lumber yard offered, and no lumber. It worked. Turnover was greater than a lumber yard or hardware store could ever dream, so margins could be reduced and still generate large profits. The broad selection drew customers. The customers knew that whatever they wanted for their home, they could find at Home Depot.

Each Home Depot was carefully located near dense middle- and upper-class residential areas. Each store generated about $34 million in sales. It was incredibly consistent.

Into this atmosphere ventured a persistent Hanes sales rep, who hit it off with the store manager, the one now walking to the front of the store. The sales rep convinced the store manager that a Hanes kiosk would fit right in and make lots of money.

It made lots of money. It was easy to put in. The Home Depot did not have to stock the kiosk or keep it orderly. That was the distributor's job. Their delivery person restacked the inventory, dusted it off, and refilled the display at least twice a week. The store manager had to do only one thing, keep the moveable kiosk within thirty feet of both a cash register and the front door.

When the manager reached the front of the store, he scrutinized the action by the kiosk. He studied the kiosk and then the woman behind the third cash register. Just an hour ago, he had asked her how the Hanes were selling. And now, $14 million.

Here's how he figured it, back in his office. She said, without batting an eye, "Oh, maybe two dozen, three dozen pair so far today. It sold better yesterday, when the kiosk was next to my register."

That estimate made the manager think that if the more-distant cash registers also sold a few pairs, they were probably moving about 75 pairs of nylons a day. That's almost $235, which makes $85,000 a year. Put that in all 160 stores and there's over $14 million in new business every year. And they were selling so fast they were paid for before the bill came due — thus, no investment.

The store manager was pumped, but he had a conservative streak so he kept this to himself. He just studied it further. He personally audited the cash-register tapes to make sure the estimates were correct. For two months he watched, all the while writing and fine-tuning a report. Sales held up. He was destined to be a $14 million hero.

Finally, he sent his report to the area office. And he waited. He knew what they would say. He just *knew* it.

He was wrong. They killed the idea. They called it "a good little business." And then they laid out their reason.

"You know," they said, "we're afraid it's going to cost us more than it makes us. It doesn't fit in."

He was incredulous.

They continued. Slowly, he began to see what they meant. The store manager, in all his excitement, had lost perspective. "What could happen here," they explained, "is that this may confuse our image. We're the Home Depot.

We should have a $10 billion business in a few years and it has been built on one thing. Homeowners come here to buy things for their home and yard. We don't sell bicycles. We don't sell candy. And we don't sell clothes, including panty hose. The truth is, we're afraid a $14 million distraction will confuse the customers and not be worth it. You know, fuzzy direction kills more businesses than competition or dying markets. We know our direction, and it doesn't include panty hose."

Fuzzy direction kills more businesses than competition or dying markets.

The people who ran the Home Depot knew what they were doing. They were quite clear about what Home Depot was, and they made sure the store manager also understood. But they weren't angry with the store manager. Quite the contrary — they applauded his initiative. And then they began to spread the story because it, as well as anything, helped define the Home Depot.

THEY TOLD OTHER store managers. They told shareholders and they told the business press, which picked up on the story. A newsletter to employees repeated the story, again praising the store manager for his initiative but repeating exactly why the Home Depot was successful. The direction was this: "Broadest selection of items anywhere for the home and yard at a fair price."

That's it. That's their flag. They raised it and they stayed with it even under the rocket's red glare of quick money.

Home Depot continues to grow 30 percent per year. Consumers recognize it as the place for selection and value.

And management repeats the story to keep the ship on course.

Here's how to hoist your flag:

1. Survey your customers, employees, and vendors. Figure out where your organization excels, or could. Decide which most-mentioned things have the greatest validity and future.

2. Put all this into several short phrases. See which stick with people. Never claim best quality, price, and service together because they are often incompatible. Pick one or two. Be specific. "At 60 miles per hour, the loudest noise is the clock," says Rolls Royce. That tells more than a tired claim like "quality." It says more than "quiet." It's specific, so it's memorable. Dominos defines its pizza service as "delivered in 30 minutes." They don't say "better," or "cheaper," or "hotter," or "spicier," or "bigger." They don't even say "quicker." They say "in 30 minutes."

3. Use the phrase in speeches, advertising, letterheads and on the front door, shipping labels, and brochures. About the time you are sick of it, others just might be starting to grasp it. Never dilute the key phrase by mentioning all the other boring things you also may do. Nobody cares. Talk to your strength.

CHAPTER 2

Specialize to Win

Doug Smith had been cursed with the worst set of blinders imaginable. He was cursed with wealth. It was a never-ending source of familial cash for the kid's company, Software Express of Big Sky, Montana. He had no perspective; he had a trust fund. And so the company grew outward, into three separate areas, but it kept losing money. Finally, after ten dreary years of losses, Dad and the family trust grew weary of waiting to win.

The board of Software Express, through a recruiter, asked me to take over as CEO.

It was interesting, but I wasn't interested. I told the recruiter that the Smith family had messed up the business for so long that failure was part of the corporate culture and that it would take drastic redirection to make the company merely break even. And then the danger was that everyone would celebrate mediocrity. "If they want to make money," I said, "they must yield all operating control."

"I don't think they're ready for that," stammered the recruiter. He cited Doug Smith's soulful commitment to the company.

Doug Smith was bright, he bristled with energy, and he could program most anything. But when it came to running a business, he didn't have a clue. His instincts never developed because he never had to worry about cash. It was like learning tennis without a net. Meaningless. He worked hard, was always enthusiastic, and usually had a grand plan *du jour.* The grand plan never had anything to do with profits. It was often a vision of new revenues, a tangent to avoid dealing with niggling details like cost, profit, and loss.

"Let them hire an eager Cub Scout," I said to the recruiter. "Let them lose another million dollars this summer. Then we'll talk."

THE DISCUSSIONS continued back and forth until finally the family trust's lawyer, in a fit of frustration, audaciously suggested it was time to cede total control of Software Express. So I joined. Doug Smith, the son, stayed and became a pal. It was impossible to dislike Doug, his unbridled enthusiasm for everything was so magnetic. But it was a disjointed attention span with no economic sense.

He had previously lasted two semesters at Montana State. He was highly intelligent and he hustled. But he flunked out. He couldn't conform. It had to do with something silly like class attendance.

Doug next worked at McDonalds in Billings, Montana. After six months, they Mcfired him. Then he moved to Big Sky, where the family trust backed him with Software Express.

As I checked out the company and talked to Doug, it was obvious that there was one thing Software Express needed to do: *less*. The company was jumping in so many directions without following through on any that it was losing money and offending customers on every front.

After twelve weeks, Doug and I talked about this and how we really could make money on any of several areas the company was in. He agreed with zeal.

I put together the new rules. There was to be no investment in any new areas for one year. There was to be a modest investment of money and more time into several existing projects. Budgets were to be set and kept. We would tighten the ship.

Doug read my proposal and liked it. The next day, he resigned, saying his talents fit better in a more entrepreneurial environment. It was good that he left. It was sad that he left.

ONE THING SOFTWARE EXPRESS produced was software that calculated mortgage amortizations for realtors and bankers. It could be customized to display tables in three different ways. These packages cost about $10,000 and took a month to customize.

The company's second product was statistical software. It had been developed at the University of Montana and was then acquired by Software Express for a royalty. This product appealed mainly to academics, and even that appeal was shaky. It cost $25,000. It was more precise and less flexible than other systems. Practical users, in quality-control departments of manufacturers, showed no interest in the product. The only people who were interested in it were bureaucratic purists. The Census Bureau and the National Institute of Health both had signed long-term leases for the software and its revisions.

The third product of Software Express was simple legal software. It sold to small law firms that wanted to computerize word processing. It was a "shelf" item — no customization required. It sold for $1,500, and display was in color. It also had the ability to print in color.

I called on several users of all three products to find out all I could on the products' appeal and weaknesses.

We discovered two competitors who made nearly identical mortgage software.

We learned that our statistical system was the best. We also learned that it was the best by only a slight margin. It was also harder to use, and it cost a lot more than the next best.

And we learned that lawyers thought it was nice that our word-processing package was the only one around in color. Not overwhelming, just nice.

We thought about improving the mortgage package over our two competitors. But they were probably thinking the same thing. And besides, that market wasn't growing. We tried anyway. We kept improving quality, and we raised prices 5 percent a month for a year. At the end of the year, 20 percent of the customers remained loyal; 80 percent told us to stuff it and left.

Those that remained were most concerned with quality, which we had improved upon each month. The 20 percent of the business that stayed was profitable, and we sold the mortgage package to a fidgety, retired banker looking for a hobby. He made more money in his next five years running this restructured business out of his den than he had in the previous thirty years at his old granite bank.

The dumbest words in business are either "full product line" or "full service."

We thought there would be an ongoing market for the statistical software if we could redesign it to make it friendlier. We decided against the redesign after seeing it would take 18 months and $250,000. Instead, we sold it to Scientific Associates, a lower-priced but stronger competitor. Scientific Associates did their own redesign and sold the package as their "Cadillac" of statistical software. It worked for them.

We renamed Software Express as Legal Rainbow. We chose to pursue the lawyers' word-processing market because, of the three original products of Software Express, only the legal package offered something of value to the customer that was unique in the market. It wasn't anything fancy that allowed us to stand completely apart. It was simply *color.* We had it, no one else did. It was our point of difference, our specialty.

Color didn't even serve a rational purpose. And our customers were lawyers — people who deal with guilt and innocence, black and white. On first glance, this may seem like the wrong group to fall for color. But color didn't serve a purpose, negative or positive. And it didn't cost any more money. Many lawyers, having analyzed every last reason to have color or not, decided to live on the edge. It was risk-free spontaneity, an attorney's dream.

SALES TRIPLED in a year. All the employees got better at color graphics because that became all Legal Rainbow did. Eighteen months later, a computer manufacturer bought the business.

I still think of Doug Smith from time to time. I hope he is doing well. His family ego got bruised a bit, but their net worth jumped several million dollars in the year and a half this took.

Legal Rainbow succeeded because it specialized. Nobody can be all things to all people. The dumbest words in business are either "full product line" or "full service." That proves the company is exceptional at nothing. Since it does more than anybody else, it does it all worse. And since it does more, it has more overhead. The lifespan for companies with poor service and high overhead is best measured by a stopwatch.

Here's how to specialize and trim the ballast from your boat:

1. Rank every product and service you sell by its gross margin. Sell off, raise prices, or shut down everything on

the bottom half of this list within a year. This takes guts. It always works.

2. Distinguish your distribution from others. If they sell to bankers, you sell to Realtors and learn their language. If they sell to Fortune 500s, you sell to Mom-and-Pop businesses. When others sell direct, cut your overhead and use sales reps. Pick one region to dominate instead of being number two or three everywhere.

3. Chart a separate course with either deeper or shallower volume discounts. If others have full product lines, narrow yours and do it better. If they offer generous terms, shave your prices and tighten up credit. Zig when they zag.

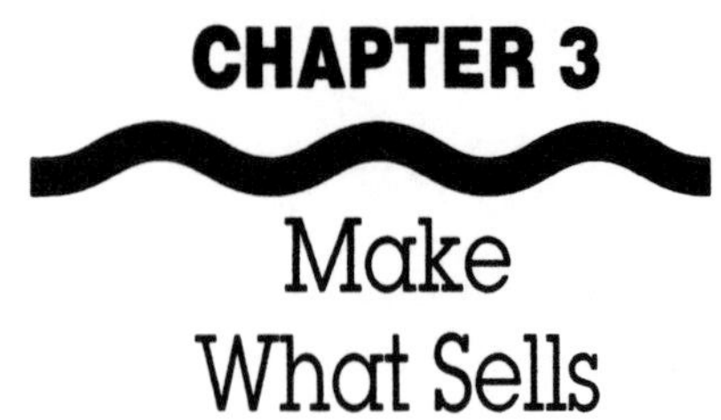

CHAPTER 3

Make What Sells

Yellow-tipped were what skies tipped me off. I was in skiing college, on a mountain actually, on vacation from Iowa State University, in Vail, Colorado with my beer-infested roommate, Willie. We were at the bottom of the slopes on our first day there when we saw the yellow tips. They seemed to swarm down the hill, carrying various shapes and sizes of skiers, all faster than we corn-fed mortals on mere wooden slats. We were in Vail for a week of skiing on our wooden Iowa skis that, in retrospect, must have looked as if they were cut from the bottom of a beer barrel next to those around us with the yellow-tipped steel skis.

The yellow-tipped skis were Head Vectors. "How can you tell?" I asked Willie, and he answered, "Look at the yellow bottoms." The new steel skis had a yellow plastic coating on the bottom and they were visible from the front because the tip curled up two inches from the snow. Thus, the yellow tips.

Howard Head, an inventor in Boulder, had developed steel skis because he thought they would sell. After two years of testing, bending and cracking prototypes on Colorado Ski Patrol volunteers, Howard Head narrowed down the formula. He figured out what temper, how thick, welded where, and just what shape to cut them. Steel, as he ultimately developed it, was lighter, springier, more consistent and quicker than wood. In 1963, he made them fly, and they blossomed like daffodils all over the Rocky Mountains. Vectors were his top-of-the-line model, and the signature of Vectors was the yellow bottom.

The yellow-tipped skis looked faster and, of course, they were race-proven. When I saw them in action, I lusted for them. I wanted faster, springier, lighter. So did everyone else, and that was proven in the market.

IT WASN'T A FAD market riding a promotional wave or a drop in pricing. The product was real. It enticed potential customers like Willie and me who went back to flat Iowa State and sat daydreaming through lectures while fashioning intricate doodles of Head skis complete with a 39-cent yellow pen to shade in the tips. I learned a lot in those lectures. I learned I really wanted to ski forever, and I reaffirmed in my signature doodle logic that it had to be on Head skis.

Companies that sell what they can make always die, but companies that make what they can sell have the formula for longevity.

Two years later, as soon as I graduated and got a job, I did buy Head skis. Everyone did. Wooden skis stacked up like cordwood in stores, even when prices were slashed and slashed again. Head skis cost four times as much as wood, and dealers couldn't keep them in stock. The Head factory was back ordered and expanded and ran their production lines three shifts a day. At one point, with some twenty companies around the world making skis, one of every three dollars spent for skis was for Heads. It was an exhilarating run, but inevitably others learned to make steel skis and Head lost some position.

Head had a trademark look — the black skis with the yellow bottom. Others came along with colors and took a little more away. But Head skis still dominated and had a strong position with almost all of its customers.

BUT THEN A EUROPEAN company, Rossignol, came along with an epoxy-composite ski. It made steel look like wood. The new skis were again faster, lighter, and stronger. Faster, lighter, and stronger won again. The new company did to Head what Head had done to the market. Head had stubbornly stuck with steel too long in the same way that many companies stick with tradition while blind to progress.

If Head had recognized sooner that steel skis were obsolete, they could have dumped the metal-stamping and metal-cutting equipment and reinvested heavily in epoxy laminates. They might have saved a large portion of their market because of customer loyalty. They probably could even have made them black with yellow bottoms.

But instead of customer loyalty, Head remained loyal to its process, believing quixotically that time and progress would stop with Head at the peak. If Head had moved forward with the market, they might not always have dominated, but they would certainly have done better than they did. It was an opportunity lost, and few even know that Head makes skis anymore.

It's easy to become inward, to get mesmerized by the stuff you are learning to do well. It's easy to not notice the world has changed directions, tastes, or desires, but a strong company must always look outward more than inward.

Companies that sell what they can make always die, but companies that make what they can sell have the formula for longevity.

To sail farther from the rocks:

1. Keep an advisory panel of customers. Get them comfortable enough so they'll criticize your directions. Listen hard for emerging threats, new concepts that are starting to do well in their minds. Rotate members on the panel each year to get fresh viewpoints. Also, gauge their business health as you go; when they are threatened by trends, so are you.

2. Set some criteria for yourself that determines when you change. If foreign sales go from 20 percent to 35 percent, do you shut down the domestic plant and move offshore? If one major chain of retailers switches from wood chair frames to plastic ones, does that prove it is time to convert the chair factory? Numerical rules (or at least guidelines) should be in place before the latest change in the marketplace. You think sharper before getting caught in a squall.

3. But never forget that hidden underneath all stated customer desires lies a never-ending urge for lower prices. This means your costs are critical, and this is the sole reason for pride in your factory or process. When your costs are below all other sources, you will win. Every time. When Head skis sold for four times the price of wooden skis, Head's costs were still below the costs of the wooden manufacturers. Head had great margins that allowed them to keep, expand, and enhance marketing, which led to more great margins. Superior cost is the only reason for loving your process.

CHAPTER 4

Cut Costs

There is a business that created itself because of an unending quest to further cut costs. It is called Price Club, and it is the product of two men with different backgrounds but the same philosophy. Cut costs.

Thirty years before the Price Club was founded, Sol Price was an attorney in San Diego. During World War II, many of his clients paid bills with their watches rather than with cash. So many clients did this, in fact, that he opened up a second-hand jewelry store. Thirty years later that store had evolved into FedMart, a chain of discount variety stores. In 1975, Price sold the company to a German retailer, Hugo Mann. Price stayed with the company as president, and the German firm sent Hans Schoepflin to be executive vice-president.

Sol Price fought the new German rigidity, such as the requirement of three signatures on every expense report. Sol fought, but it wasn't his company anymore. Sol lost; he was fired.

Hans Schoepflin became president of FedMart, and Sol opened a new business called Price Club. Sol also sued FedMart, Mann, and Schoepflin for breach of contract.

Sol leased a warehouse in a commercial area ten minutes from my home in La Jolla, California, just north of

San Diego. "Nobody came," Sol recalls. "After six months we had to decide whether to put some more money in to keep it going."

The Price Club eliminated middlemen, sales clerks, and excessive handling. It was a warehouse. Customers helped themselves to huge quantities for incredible discounts. For instance, those panty hose that Home Depot wouldn't touch in Chapter 1 were sold at Price Club for $25 a ten-pack. It worked here; it was win-win.

BUT FOR THE FIRST six months, the concept was dormant. There were few customers and lots of inventory. Sol and a few other friendly investors were $750,000 into it. At six months, he didn't hesitate — he decided to go ahead and invest another $250,000. No more. He still doesn't know why. Just a feeling, something instinctive. Whatever, he was right. Customers finally started coming.

> Hardly ever are business people blessed with a market so strong or isolation so great that price is unrelated to cost.

Maybe the few customers they had at the beginning began talking. Maybe word of mouth moved slow in the balmy weather of southern California. There is no explanation for the delay in success. But there is an explanation for the success — customers love to save money.

For three years, Sol and Hans never talked, but they met regularly in courtooms and lawyers' offices. Sol listened intently to every deposition Hans gave in the lawsuit, and over time it became clear they shared the same philosophy.

About three years after the split, Hans sensed Sol was

right and his home-country owners were wrong. This wasn't Germany. This was San Diego. Beards were fine. Jeans were okay. Even suits and ties were all right, if not overdone. What wasn't good were stupid rules. Hans knew, as Price had said, there should be only one rule: cut costs. But Hugo Mann wanted to expand.

Hans lost, too, so he quit. About the same time, the lawsuit was settled.

IN THE SUMMER of 1978, Sol asked Hans to come work for him. They met for coffee and discussed a shared belief that reducing distribution costs was critical to success. That system required low-rent warehouses, all palletized racks, and forklift direct loading of merchandise from the truck onto the sales floor.

They kept talking. Retailing is fun, they agreed, and deep discounting is the wave of the future. It was so easy. Sol Price was depression-scarred and cost-conscious. Hans Schoepflin was a CPA by trade: he saw every cost as an evil and he never saw a necessary evil. They looked at retailing from a new perspective, moving an entire step up the food chain of retailing.

According to Sol Price, it works because of limited selection and large containers. Accounting is easier, inventory is easier, and best of all, fewer customers buy more of the product. Price says, "Losing customers pays."

Price describes it this way: "Suppose 10,000 customers walk through in a day. Assume ten need some light oil for around the house. If you carry a 12-ounce can, an 8-ounce can, and a 3-ounce can, you'll sell oil to ten customers.

"One buys the 12-ounce can, three buy the 8-ounce can, and six buy the 3-ounce can. Add it up. You've sold ten customers 54 ounces of oil by stocking three sizes.

"But at the Price Club, we might only carry the 12-ounce can. Half of the ten buyers won't buy. It's too much oil. So we sell five, and at 12 ounces each we've just sold 60 ounces. But the best part is, now we get a deeper discount from the oil company. They have to ship only one size to the Price Club. Plus, we are selling more. So the customer gets a break. And now we sell even more oil with a lower price yet. That's how losing customers pays, and everybody wins."

The Price Club earns deep price cuts from suppliers for making their life easier with less packaging. If suppliers refuse, that category is not carried. It keeps a sense of discovery in shopping.

It works so well that Price Club has no inventory expense. Items sell in two weeks or they are not reordered. Vendor payment is usually due in thirty days. Most products sell in half that time.

When the customers started to come to Price Club, more outlets were opened. *Forbes* magazine picked it as the most profitable growth company of the 1980s. Sales in 1992 passed $7 billion. That's not bad growth for the first 16 years. Profits are up again in 1993. It looks as if they'll make it. They are still looking to cut costs.

When Sol Price asked Hans Schoepflin to join Price Club in 1978, Hans accepted a nominal salary and stock options. That stock became worth $100 million within a decade.

Even after the company made millionaires out of anybody who invested $2500 in the early years, the annual report was still done on a copying machine.

Success bred competitors. Costco and Sam's Clubs appeared. They, too, became multibillion dollar operations in a few years. Everybody won.

What Sol and Hans knew on their way to the megamillionaires club is that there is no such thing as a fixed cost. No savings is trivial. Each sets an example, and rarely is there a motivating feature stronger than finding the best price. Hardly ever are business people blessed with a market so strong or isolation so great that price is unrelated to cost. Cost reduction, therefore, is the greatest market-developing activity that exists.

Sooner or later every washed-up, burnt-out marketing executive like myself starts to realize that accountants, those shy bean counters, have always been a bit better at questioning and reducing costs than we flashy marketing guys. Therefore, accountants are better marketers than we marketers.

A lighter hull moves faster in every wind. Here's how your crew can trim weight:

1. Cut management salaries by 5 percent. Drop CEO and vice-president salaries 10 percent. Add monthly profit bonuses based on profits. When monthly profits meet last year's, give a 10 percent bonus. Watch requests for expenditures drop. This gets everybody rowing in the same direction.

2. Put together a new committee each month to come up with new cost reductions. Use a cross-section of employees. Pay for their time and give them 30 days to deliver the five most important cost reductions possible and then publish the recommendations each month. Post a list of all suggestions actually used along with committee members' names. Split 20 percent of the first year's savings among the committee members.

3. Set an example yourself. Use excursion air fares, schedule Saturday travel meetings to drop hotel and air fares, and check alternative long-distance services. Cut back the trash and janitorial service, buy used furniture and office equipment, move your office to a cheaper location, and put in more plants and brighter paint. Organize purchasing so everything costing more than $1,000 is bought on bid.

Finally, stop replacing departed employees for 180 days and see what happens. Your remaining employees might prefer keeping the work themselves and getting better profit bonuses.

CHAPTER 5

Energize New Product Plans

When Kodak announced its 110 Instamatic camera at a photo show in Chicago, we at Honeywell felt we had to develop our own. You didn't have to be a Rhodes Scholar to figure out the 110 would sell; it fit into a shirt pocket and took excellent pictures.

We were inspired by competition. We were inspired by fear. We would meet at work, after work, in a bar or in the bowling alley. We became obsessed, but something interesting happened. We began to talk about more than just the camera. "What if," somebody in our little group asked, "we could somehow make it focus automatically?"

It was as if we stumbled on it, just by talking about it. "It" — automatic focus — became a secondary obsession but one that was grander. The 110 had already been built. And although our main goal was to make a better 110 camera, we found our real energy going on a tangential run to automatic focus. It became part of our consciousness.

I was the director of product management. Dean Peterson was the head of the mechanical engineering section for Honeywell's photo-products division. I remember one moment when Dean stood among us near his drafting table after a particularly futile discussion and suddenly he flung his drafting pen and it stuck about a half inch into the accoustical tiling on the wall. "We've got to do something different," he barked. "There's nothing breakthrough here, there's nothing here that is going to move the world even one degree."

Peterson was a big talent at a small division of Honeywell. It was as if Barishnikov had been hired to call a square dance, yet Peterson flourished at Honeywell because of his freedom. Peterson, who had already designed the first instamatic camera at Kodak before coming to Honeywell, was driven by nightmares of becoming average and, thus, so were we.

THE IDEA WAS to design a camera but, really, everyone kept thinking about the possibility of automatic focus. Peterson had three other engineers working on it. Their names were Stauffer, Wilwerding, and Ogawa. They and I met every day for eighteen months, but they were intentionally isolated from the rest of the company. Finally, at the end we had a good camera, but it was 8 percent over the budget. With teary eyes, we killed it.

But sometime during those eighteen months, we figured out the essence of focus. None of us remembers the exact moment so it wasn't like a light bulb over someone's head or even a grand vision. It was just a lot of brainwork and discussions.

Focus, we figured out, is nothing more than the moment of maximum contrast. It was easy to measure contrast by sprinkling light meters all over the image and measuring the contrast between them. If the lens started at infinity (with a gray image and zero contrast) and then started moving until the moment of maximum contrast, focus would be achieved.

When we scrapped the camera, we realized that automatic focus was still possible, so we persuaded Honeywell to invest another $85,000 to prove it further. We had already invested $15,000, so that brought the total investment up to $100,000.

It took another eight months to build a working prototype, and then it was assigned to a separate marketing group that went about making presentations to other companies. Every camera manufacturer was interested, but some didn't believe a disheveled little band of Rocky Mountain engineers could make something as earth shattering as automatic focus. Many refused to pay royalties.

EIGHTEEN YEARS LATER, after testimony from Peterson, Ogawa, Stauffer, Wilwerding, and myself, one of those companies, Minolta, handed Honeywell a check for $127 million for past royalties due. There are others — Kodak, Canon, Sony, and more — due to settle with Honeywell. All in all, it should amount to just under $1 billion in total royalties. That's not bad — $1 billion profit on a $100,000 investment.

If you can't write a compelling headline, the product is no good.

It is the biggest royalty award in American history.

It's funny thinking back to that time. Honeywell was in a funk, having lost much of the electronic flash market to Vivitar and being threatened with the loss of the Pentax line. There were other problems too, like a slide projector that wouldn't sell.

When we set out to build a new 110 camera, we had a new rule that helped direct product development: "Before spending a dime, write the announcement headline in 25 words or less." Half the pending projects were immediately stillborn. It's startling how much dumb development can be exposed by that test. If you can't write a compelling headline, the product is no good. Honeywell found a new compass, and that compass led to autofocus. One billion dollars in profits resulted.

Here is how to magnetize your compass:

1. Put tight direction into research and development. Write the announcement headline with specific, unique benefits. Review precise dates, expenditures, and progress for each project weekly. Then get out of the engineers' way. Focus on the project in every business report you issue. Profits are history. The new product is your future.

2. Stay loose and re-examine unexpected breakthroughs. Development can and must be scheduled. It not only leads to progress on the stated project, but it can also lead to unthought-of spinoffs that hardly ever come from aimless tinkering. Honeywell's pocket camera was killed, but autofocus came from a scheduled camera.

3. Isolate the design crew. Let them have no other mission or distraction. Make their careers hinge on success and terminate projects when they miss major benchmarks.

CHAPTER 6

Manage More Than Lead

Three men and three car companies. Two companies lost money. One made money.

It was January 1982 in San Diego when it hit me. Certainly, Detroit's been the "Bad News Bears" of the 80's and 90's. Here's my spin. Roger Smith, chairman of General Motors, was to speak at the San Diego Advertising Club. I was invited. I stood outside talking to the president of the club when a massive black tractor trailor backed its way under the awning of the Hilton. I'd heard and seen the General Motors slogan a million times before, but this was the first time it really registered. On the side of the huge black trailor, it said, "General Motors Mark of Excellence."

Inside, there was another crew already in place. They unloaded a second truckload of audio visual equipment, set up and tested it. They came out for this next load.

The president of the advertising club turned to me with a wry smile. "We knew he was already scheduled to talk in L.A. We knew January in San Diego is better than January in Detroit. So we gave it a shot and look, two trucks."

Two trucks for one speech by one man.

The Mark of Excellence.

It was a breath-quickening presentation — rhythmic drumbeats and trumpets blasted through the stereo as the screen dramatically came to life. Smith talked about the new Saturn project, advertising for the coming year, and how wonderful General Motors was now that he, Smith, was in charge.

SMITH, ONCE AN INTROVERTED financial guy, loved to give a speech. Besides two truckloads of audio-visual equipment, Smith came with an entourage of P.R. flaks who made lots of money communicating superfluous anecdotes about their boss, Smith. This beat any Broadway show. It was staged to inspire, and we in surf's-up San Diego were awed. We were in America. And after all, what's good for General Motors is good for America.

Right?

Detroit is in America too. That's the thing. You see, I was impressed by the speech. The guy got my heart pumping when he talked about the Saturn project and its vast potential. He spoke for thirty minutes while this huge, imported-from-Detroit wall-to-wall, ceiling-to-floor video screen flashed professional graphics and photographs illustrating every point. Lights were arranged so that Smith's diminutive profile became incandescent in the muted convention room. Often, the giant screen flashed an image of a giant Saturn logo. This was three-dimensional audio-visual turbo-glide charisma.

I sat in wonder, and then an image flashed into my mind. It was one of the out-of-nowhere loose connections we all make.

I thought of Lee Iacocca, president of Chrysler. He is far more famous than Smith. A leader. What he is famous for are two books, his starring bill in Chrysler television commercials, and his role in raising money to refurbish the Statue of Liberty.

That year, both General Motors and Chrysler lost money. Lots of money. General Motors laid off 12,000 workers and cut the bonuses of most remaining workers. Except top executives, of course. The privileged class, each with two commas on their W–2s, all received bonuses for a job well done. It seemed their bonuses were for helping sell Smith's strategy. What else could they be for? Results?

THERE WAS ONE GUY who stayed in Detroit that year. Donald Peterson never wrote a book or starred in a commercial. He tried his best to give no speeches and those he did were mostly in Detroit. His talks cured insomnia. Peterson was unassuming and had no desire for the spotlight. He only wanted better cars first, and he assumed profits would follow. Never heard of Peterson? He was CEO of Ford.

Leadership is seductive.
Management is work.

His philosophy was simple. He told his designers to forget about profits and instead design something they would like to see in their own driveways.

Ford had a slogan too: "Quality Is Job One." Quality became the mission of the company, and Ford's quality, by most standards, soon passed General Motors and Chrysler. Incidentally, so did profits. No contest.

Peterson retired and was replaced by another hands-on guy you've never heard of, Red Poling. And in 1992 Poling's new Taurus became the number-one seller in America.

While Ford thrives, introducing the Taurus and Sable, good cars with record profits, General Motors and Chrysler falter — losing huge amounts and a dozen plants.

What hit home that day as Roger Smith put on his traveling jamboree was that this was the most fraudulent of all skills — leadership without management. He was like some snake-oil huckster spinning yarns about the joyous culture of General Motors and its success. But, of course, it was a promise from another empty suit without follow-through. The scariest thing is he probably believed what he said. He was isolated, obviously unaware that only leadership by example works.

Leadership is necessary but leadership is seductive — a massage for the ego. I've tasted it on a tiny scale myself. When I have been CEO of various companies, vendors, customers, and old associates who should know better have become ridiculously deferential. My jokes were just as bad, but the laughter got louder. It's easy to lose perspective.

Management is work. Management is listening and digging for problems.

I ONCE ASKED a sampling of CEOs of both large and small companies which task they preferred, giving a speech to new employees or participating in a customer negotiation. The CEOs of large companies preferred to give the speech. The small-company CEOs wanted to negotiate. The way I see it, large companies are laying people off, small companies are getting some work done, growing and hiring.

Leaders deliver impressions and play to the desires of the masses. Managers inspire less and accomplish more. Think about how many great Japanese business leaders you can name. What are they like personally? There aren't many inspiring the masses. They are too busy managing their businesses, working. They know how business really works.

Ahab and Captain Queeg were leaders; their crews barely survived. Here's how to keep the captain's galley from becoming more important than the rigging and sails:

1. Any employee who always agrees with you is redundant. Replace him or her with someone who will contribute.

2. Eliminate public speeches except when it helps business. Speak, when you must, in front of smaller groups

where you can ask questions and listen. Listeners win; talkers lose.

3. If the choice is between settling an employee dispute or meeting with the Chamber of Commerce, get with the employees. If a disgruntled customer wants to see you, cancel that supplier luncheon. Given the choice between symbolic acts and work, do the work. That's symbolic in itself.

CHAPTER 7

Know the Customer

In 1982, when software sales across the country were skyrocketing, State of the Art software was a new company. State of the Art made accounting software. Their first-year sales were $1 million, and their second year was $3 million. The third-year sales rate hit $10 million, and all along net profits were an unheard-of 30 percent.

Franklin Press printed the instruction manuals and documentation that go with the software and was constantly rushed by State of the Art to put everything else aside and attend to their emergency orders.

Late one Friday, Polly, the no-nonsense buyer from State of the Art, barked at Karen, the Franklin Press sales rep.

"Karen, we need them Monday," said Polly in a tone of voice that defied her 4'11" frame. Polly glared. "Monday. Period."

Karen pleaded, "But if you could just give us a one-week lead time, we could save you 50 percent."

But Karen didn't get it. It was the opulent early eighties and software was chic, as was life. State of the Art had contemporary glass offices with a swirling modern art sculpture exploding like a new idea in their lobby. The founders were energetic and determined. They worked fourteen-hour days, six days a week. On the seventh, they played extravagently.

THE CEO WAS particularly smitten. Newly rich, he wanted to recapture his youth. He hired a private investigator to track down that nostalgia; the investigator was hired to find the exact '59 maroon Ford Fairlaine he cruised in during high school. It was located. The CEO bought the old car, refurbished it, and had it stored in the company warehouse as a shrine to his youth.

"Hey, you don't understand," Polly, the buyer, told Karen. Despite Polly's diminutive size, she could be heard in the next zip code. She had frazzled hair, no makeup. She looked tough, acted tough, was tough — a graduate of the business streets of New York. "That ink and paper costs us only $8 a set. We sell it, with the disk, for $500 and we're back ordered. Eight dollars is nothing. I can't afford to be a day late just to save $4. We need it now!"

Customers often act for the moment without thinking of their longer-term wants. Sometimes they don't understand what they are doing to themselves.

It was delivered the following Monday. Franklin's bindery worked Saturday, Saturday night, and Sunday. The customer paid twice too much and was happy. But Karen went back the following week and made another pitch. She didn't have to make another pitch, and, in fact, many companies wouldn't have approved. They would take the extra money and run. They would be wrong.

Karen told Polly, "You are making a lot of money, but we're shipping you $12,000 worth of printed material in an average month. Look at this. If you could just, for five minutes every Monday, forecast your needs with me for a couple of weeks running, I could cut $6,000 in rush fees out of your monthly bill."

"But . . ."

"Look, I know you are back ordered and making huge profits. But for just five minutes a week you could save $6,000 a month. That's not trivial."

The buyer, even in her gruffness, understood. A lesser salesperson wouldn't have bothered. But Karen looked out for the buyer's interest, even when the buyer didn't.

STATE OF THE ART finally did understand and they tightened their ship. Sales continued up and profits did even better. In 1990 they went public. Polly had survived a cutback forced on the company by the temporary slump of 1984. She might have been let go if she had had sloppier buying practices. Instead, she went on to earn stock that became worth $250,000.

At the time of this incident, State of the Art was wildly successful, and so was Polly. But neither the company nor the buyer was so awed by success that they wouldn't listen to a sales rep talking sense.

State of the Art remained successful, even in tough times, because they were willing to listen. It is now the only PC-based accounting software company that's publicly held. They had sales of $30 million in 1992. It appears they will make, after taxes, a profit of $10 million.

Karen, the sales rep, also enhanced her career. Within three years she became dissatisfied with being a printing sales rep and formed her own brokerage business, representing many printers and calling on the same customers.

Much of Karen's success came from old-fashioned hustle. She always made more calls than her competitive sales reps, thus learning more about her customers and their needs. She understood the economics of printing and her customers' business, often better than the customers themselves. She learned never to keep her mouth shut, and she knew that the customer is sometimes wrong.

Customers often act for the moment without thinking of their longer-term wants. Sometimes they don't understand what they are doing to themselves. You must know them better than they know themselves so you can deliver to their deeper desires without offending them.

Here's how to keep your crew and passengers from capsizing in swells of success:

1. Take a look at your special orders. Nothing enobles a supplier more than exceptional emergency service. You must do this to save customers. But they should pay extra because nothing kills a supplier more quickly than delivering a superior service without charging for it. Many won't see it as a special unless it is priced as such.

2. Stop any discounts given for shoddy product or poor service. Replace or redo it, and do it right. Customers who are delighted with discounts and lousy service are lethal.

3. Cut your commission schedule in half. Enhance it with bonuses based on customer interviews, repeat purchases, and displaced competitors. This is tough to administer, but the resulting arguments are more relevant than any you've had yet.

CHAPTER 8

Buy Low

When Frank March bid on the contract to build replacement urethane bumpers that protect the piers of the San Pedro, California, shipyard, he was already $77,000 ahead of his competitors.

March's plant manager in Virginia had just paid $5,000 for a urethane sprayer at a bankruptcy auction. Along with the functional motor and gadgetry, there were some rusty pipes and cracked hoses. It was part of the deal. March spent another $3,000 to treat the rust and replace the hoses. Then it performed like new, for a total of $8,000.

All the competitors, however, had shiny new sprayers, for $85,000. They didn't get any rust or cracked hoses, but Frank March got a $77,000 head start. The San Pedro project was awarded in its entirety to March's company, Seaward International. All the other companies found less work and higher payments for those expensive, shiny sprayers.

MARCH IS ONE of those completely directional people, who knew before he scored a perfect 800 on his math SATs that science and business and life are logical. He went to MIT, became class president, advised the Harvard COOP store, and eventually finished with a bachelor's degree in chemical engineering and a masters in oceanographic sciences. His direction was set — the chemical engineer in him made a chemical product for the oceanographer in him. Logic goes straight forward for March.

For instance, equipment savings such as the sprayer add up to roughly 2 percent a year. "It's a goal, and we meet it," said March. "Every year, in new ways."

Bumpers for ships look easy but are tough to design and even tougher to improve. A perfect combination of flotation and resilience without flex-fatigue is needed to protect both the ship and the pier. The bumper must give just enough to protect it, without giving so much it will crumble prematurely. Certain proprietary combinations of varying urethane layers make Seawards' bumpers more effective than any others, and seasoned mariners know it.

March always buys low. Seaward bought an abandoned paper mill for its factory in rural Clearbrook, Virginia. The price was right and labor is good. More important, the isolation protects the secrecy of most projects.

The problem with accounting is that you can overspend and capitalize it, and the results don't show up for years.

The money saved by buying used and abandoned facilities went toward progress — factory automation. In an industry built on cheap labor (many companies use untrained immigrant labor), hand processing, and inconsistant results, Seaward is computer-driven and automated.

March is involved everywhere. "We spend the better part of a year programming the trimmer that cuts sheets precisely for each size bumper," he said. "That is one year's work but it is worth it. We now use 50 percent more of what we used to throw away as scrap. That's a savings of

3 percent. A 3 percent price advantage gains us 10 percent more sales. It just goes on and on, how cutting leads to earning. The 10 percent volume increase lets us negotiate urethane prices down further." It is wonderful to watch costs go down while volume and profits go up. It is self-perpetuating.

The few customers who have seen Seaward inside advised competitors to simply drop out of the business. Most competitors took heed. A few, like Yokohama, plug on but lag miserably. Yokohama, DuPont, and others have new sprayers. Some have new buildings. Seaward, though, has new customers.

March is smart enough to know that money is money — not something to play with by using accounting. The problem with accounting is that you can overspend and capitalize it, whether it is equipment or an acquisition, and the results don't show up for years. It gives businesses a fuse that is too long. When you hear, "That's okay, we'll just capitalize it," you know you're in a sick management environment that is hiding costs using perfectly proper accounting.

Trim your provisioning bill at dockside by doing this:

1. Never buy new equipment unless it's more productive per-dollar-spent than refurbished. Don't buy even refurbished if you can have outside sources do it for less.

2. Examine every service or part you manufacture. See if it can be bought cheaper than it costs you to make it. If so, stop doing it yourself. Doing it yourself does not "maintain control." If you can buy it cheaper than you can make it, you lost "control" of that process a long time ago. Next you will lose customers if you continue to make it.

3. Never acquire a company unless you can see a complete payoff in five years based on their current earnings. More acquisitions fail than succeed. The inherent inefficien-

cies of mixing organizations into an unspecialized blob is one reason for failure. The primary reason acquisitions fail, though, is that the buyer simply paid too much.

CHAPTER 9

Sell High

This was white-knuckle time.

About a year earlier, Smiley Industries, which I now ran, won the contract to make part of the transmission housings for the Apache helicopter. The overall contractor for the Apache was McDonnell Douglas. They awarded us the subcontract.

Like all government contracts, this was politics and bureaucracy. First of all, the reason the contract went out to bid was because of politics. Once, there was one contractor making all three parts of the housings. But in an effort to spread the wealth among more congressional districts, the housing parts were bid separately. It made sense — politically.

Practically, however, it made life miserable. The previous contractor who had made all three parts had flexibility to mix and match, as long as it worked. But now, each contractor had to make each part precisely according to specifications. This sounds fair. But you should have seen the specifications.

It was humiliating. Perhaps a smarter outfit than we were could have figured this out by thinking harder while studying the blueprints. There were, however, a lot of other dumb bidders on this job.

The thing that threw us off was the use of an unusual

alloy — titanium, nickel, and steel — in a shape larger than normal. When we machined this larger part at an economic speed, it created vibrations that made it virtually impossible to create dimensions within the required 1/10,000 of an inch. At economical machining speeds, the vibrations caused scuffed and chipped surfaces that couldn't quite meet specifications.

The more we tried, the more we struggled. We fell four months behind, and our cash was squeezed as a result. We hadn't yet figured out the problem. We thought it must be doable. After all, somebody was making these parts before.

Yes, but somebody was making all these parts and playing matchmaker, switching parts that were just off the mark until they fit. We now had no such luxury.

At one point, a McDonnell Douglas officer visited. He brought with him a gaggle of managers and clipboards. He explained his dilemma and blamed it on us. "Mr. Sutton," he said, "40 percent of NATO's helicopters are grounded today due to your failure to deliver." He was right. We had failed to deliver.

But he, of course, hadn't explained that the previous supplier couldn't meet the specs either. He didn't say a word about mix-and-match manufacturing. We had to figure out that part for ourselves.

We did finally get it. But it didn't help any. All it did was convince us we had made a bad bid.

In all fairness, McDonnell Douglas probably didn't realize what was happening either. They were just frustrated and mad. Their attitude seemed, even to us, justifiable.

AFTER TWO MORE MONTHS of stumbling and cursing, we finally found an adequate solution. We used a sharper cutting tool at a higher speed. It took a while even to find the exact speed. We set the "bite" for a thinner cut. Then we had to clamp a set of weights onto certain parts of each piece while we machined it. This helped dampen the vibration. It worked, but there was a problem. A rather significant problem. This new procedure took twice as much effort as our bid indicated.

We went to McDonnell Douglas and explained the problem.

"So what do you want us to do?" asked the McDonnell Douglas officer.

"You have no choice," I said. "You have to double our price per part." His eyes bulged. I continued. "Your other alternative is to go somewhere else."

"You do realize you have a binding contract," he pointed out.

It was a fight to get everyone to realize just how underpriced these parts were. There was a natural, yet irrational fear of losing the contract.

I nodded. "Yes," I said, "and we've done everything humanly possible to honor it. Together, we've discovered a problem neither of us knew we had with this part. It's not your fault, it's not our fault. But it is a problem. A major problem. And we've figured out how to make it a much better part than you ever had before. Now it truly is interchangeable for the first time. That will slash your field repair costs. Unfortunately, we can't make it on the terms of that contract. We're sorry, but it is such a big contract that we would go bankrupt trying to honor it as is. If you choose to force us, you will be dealing with a creditor committee when you want a spare part for NATO."

McDonnell Douglas relented. They even agreed to pay

some advances to cover prior excessive costs due to the problem. It turned out well. The project lived, Smiley made better parts at fair profit, and NATO's forces remained at the ready.

BUT THE BIGGER POINT of the story was in the real battle. Inside Smiley it was a fight to get everyone to realize just how underpriced these parts were. There was a natural, yet irrational fear of losing the contract. There was not enough appreciation that we would lose our entire business if we honored the existing contract. McDonnell Douglas, with plenty of encouragement, did the right thing and Smiley Industries survived.

This was a price increase that was fair and correct, yet if put to either an employee or management vote the approach would probably have been more humble. The result of a humble approach might have been that McDonnell Douglas would never have fully realized the problem. If Smiley had wobbled and failed, McDonnell Douglas would have had the same problem all over again with some other unlucky bidder. And Apache helicopters could have been a repair disaster, struggling to stay on-line, without interchangeable parts.

Price increases are often necessary. They force scrutiny, which is healthy. It isn't always pleasant, but when there's a problem, nothing flushes out reality quicker.

Here's how to keep the boat full with passengers paying fair fares:

1. Raise prices by 10 percent on each product and service that isn't making money. See what happens. Some customers will be unfazed, and then the product is profitable. With other increases, you will lose some business but probably make money with the customers that are left. And with some, it will kill sales entirely. All three results are good. You've separated the winners from the losers.

2. Take the items that died with a 10 percent price increase and reintroduce them with a 25 percent cut. See if the increased volume makes it a winner. Watch closely and be ready to kill it instantly if it doesn't work, which it often won't.

3. Sugarcoat the price increases. Somehow, a chocolate mint on a pillow makes an overpriced hotel room a little more acceptable. Your customers aren't dumb, but it's rude not to make it easier for them to swallow price increases.

PART 2

THE CREW: Boosting Personnel Productivity

CHAPTER 10

Make Personnel Personal

As a maker of exhibits for trade shows and retail displays, Pacific Design Center had vast potential and opportunity. It was the biggest exhibit design center on the West Coast, but financial results were below mediocre.

At Pacific Design Center, the personnel department was too big and overbearing. When I was hired as CEO, there were nine full-time personnel people, each of whom had enough time to get in *everybody's* way.

For one thing, there was the manager's manual, an encyclopedic-looking thing with dry jargon-filled text and a red-white-and-blue cover. It probably took days for a committee to pick out the the colors for the cover. The text was picky, diminutive, and full of invasive, self-defeating techniques for "motivating" workers and management. There wasn't much in that stack of pages that had to do with anything produced by Pacific Design Center.

For another thing, there were the evalution forms — eight pages of unimportant nosy drivel that once again had almost nothing to do with results. There were 500 employees at the company, and one evalution form had to be filled out annually by every supervisor for every employee. That's 4,000 pages produced, and nothing gained.

Once a quarter, the personnel department held half-day training sessions with other managers, teaching them to manage better. That's two solid days of work a year for every manager, and nothing gained.

The nine personnel people had so little to do they actually went out finding studies showing that it was average to have nine personnel people for a company of 500 employees. Who were the studies done by? The American Personnel Association. That's who gained.

One month after I arrived, despite all these manuals, training sessions, and forms, a forklift tipped over and destroyed a builder's exhibit for the Home & Garden Show. A couple of weeks later a worker lost control of his sabersaw, and it severed a nerve in his wrist.

There were more problems. There were five trade unions, which tells a lot about how labor felt about management. Lots of employees seemed to come down with the "Monday-morning flu" and three fourths of the worker's compensation claims were filed before 10 A.M. Monday, showing that even those who came in Monday morning weren't ready for work, and their claims were less than valid.

If you just walked around and kept your eyes open, especially in the bathrooms, you knew there was a drug problem at Pacific Design Center. You could sense things, see things, hear things, sometimes smell things that the managers never noticed because they were distracted by filling out forms.

The final straw came after I had been there two months. We were holding a meeting of managers in my office, just going around so each could give an update on what was happening in his or her department. When it came to the personnel manager's turn, she gushed, "There's so much pain out there!" Her body language hit about three major cheerleading poses. "We've started holding anonymous lunchtime meetings for people with personal problems. All kinds, any kinds. There are people hurting out there. We get them to talk, to really let go. Just yesterday, we had two people crying."

She was into this. The more depression, the better.

We listened to her, and we made some changes. One of the best changes we made was cutting the personnel department in half.

Suddenly, managers had to manage again. If an employee wasn't performing, the manager had to discuss it before salary-review time, instead of overlooking it and later blaming a small raise on the personnel department.

Suddenly, those left in personnel were busy without intruding on others. The business flourished. Managers and employees talked to one another honestly, and raises were no longer cloaked in secrecy.

Don't create a new rule or policy every time somebody screws up.

We didn't fire the people in personnel. We found them jobs where they could be productive — in sales and production. You see, they weren't lazy but they had a predisposition to forms, lectures, organizational charts, and structure like name plates and titles. They adapted well when put into meaningful jobs.

SIX MONTHS LATER, everyone in management and supervision could see the decision to reduce the personnel department was correct. Six months after that, we did it again, reducing a five-member personnel department to three. And things got better yet.

Productivity jumped. Costs for similar work from the previous year dropped by an average of 10 percent. In that year, in fact, productivity savings were roughly $850,000.

There was a tradeoff. Pacific Design Center lost a couple of wrongful termination suits that cost about $45,000. That's a nice tradeoff for $850,000 in savings, eh?

The truth is, the minute you create a department to tell the managers how to manage, you are automatically telling them to manage less. You are diffusing responsibility.

Don't do it. Set the people free. Let managers manage and make some mistakes; it's good for them and for your company. Don't create a new rule or policy every time somebody screws up. In fact, beware the employee who never makes a mistake. There is something to learning to take chances.

Here's how to sail faster by reducing meaningless drills:

1. Cut your personnel department in half. Find those you cut other jobs within the company since growing a personnel department was your error, not theirs.

2. One year later, do it again. Yes, it is possible, and, yes, things will get better yet.

3. Create a philosophy of rewards for performance with your employees that all understand and write together. Don't let this degenerate into rules or formulas, but make it a clear manifesto that everybody gets a copy of when they join the company. Build the framework together from which individual judgments and actions can be made independently.

CHAPTER 11

Pursue Productive People

In July 1963, Jim Kennedy was hired by George Van Auken to work for one day. Kennedy was hired by Van Auken, who owned Franklin Press in San Bernardino, California, to haul 500 bundles of insurance brochures to a client an hour away in Anaheim.

At the time, Kennedy was 20 years old — a "kid" to Van Auken. After Kennedy pulled up in his red pickup, they talked briefly about the order and then the two of them loaded the truck. Van Auken worked hard carrying and stacking the bundles in the back of the truck, but Kennedy loaded twice as many and he was meticulous — staggering the second row of bundles so the load wouldn't shift.

The entire time, Kennedy was effusive, holding a fluid conversation, sometimes just with himself, and using his eyes and hands as well as his vocal chords to communicate. He was upbeat.

So Van Auken asked him, "How long you been working for this delivery service?"

"About two years," said Kennedy, who still didn't stop, although he did slow down at the question — just a little. "Why?"

"Well, would you like to work in printing?"

"Is that an offer?"

"Yes."

Van Auken reasoned it like this: Anybody who works that hard and that good can work for me.

And so Jim Kennedy drove that load to Anaheim and then gave his notice at the trucking company. Two weeks later, Jim Kennedy went to work full time for George Van Auken.

GEORGE VAN AUKEN never checked a reference in his life, he never gave a personality test, and he hardly ever advertised for employees. He went looking. He was always looking because he believed that his employees were his company. His was a strong company because of this.

When he had his car gassed up, he observed the gas station attendant who smiled and took care washing his windshield. If a CPA did a quicker-than-normal auditing job and asked questions that he hadn't thought of, Van Auken remembered. He had mental files on dozens of potential employees — people who had never worked in printing. He didn't care; he just waited for openings. He told them when he hired them, "I can teach you to be a printer. I can't teach what's inside of you. That's the part I hired."

He built Franklin Press one person at a time and then twelve years after Van Auken hired Kennedy, he sold the company. I was hired to manage the company. Not that it needed it.

"I can teach you to be a printer. I can't teach what's inside of you. That's the part I hired."

By the time Van Auken sold the company, Kennedy had long since risen to run the shipping department. It is still his job today. More than once during my two years at the company, Kennedy came to me with a suggestion that helped productivity and customer relations. Often it was as simple as getting a partial shipment out before the end of the month. Almost always, the suggestion helped the customer and the company.

Even when Van Auken was gone from the company, his spirit lived on through Kennedy and all the employees he had hired. I just sat back and enjoyed it. One Halloween, one of our drivers dressed up as a gorilla and did twelve deliveries — driving 200 miles — in gorilla character. Unsolicited, we heard from all twelve customers. They all loved it. This was the spirit that Van Auken hired. He nurtured a team concept as he built his business from the inside of his garage into a modern printer pulling in $10 million in business in a year.

He hired a dairyman who knew how to work a route. He made the dairyman a salesman, and the new salesman built up loyal clientele because of his consistent follow-up. He hired another kid out of high school and that kid rose to production foreman over 100 tradesmen at Franklin Press.

The legacy continued for many because the "can-do" spirit was encouraged. The kid out of high school eventually cashed out and opened up a bar. The dairyman wasn't an entrepreneur but he knew what he wanted and he had the means to get it. When he retired, he moved with his wife to the lush fairways, pools, and dry desert air of Palm Springs.

Many of the original people are gone today but Franklin Press remains a stalwart printer. It is bigger than ever because it delivers more consistently with better productivity than its competitors. Average tenure is greater at Franklin. Turnover is below 10 percent per year, and employees are energetic and spontaneous.

George Van Auken set out to build more than a business of numbers and products; he knew the foundation was the people and the culture they created. The culture of Franklin Press was pride and dedication, just as George Van

Auken envisioned and sought out.

Here's how to find good crew members in all walks of life:

1. Keep in touch with the best people you know as vendors, customers, and competitors. Woo them. Get to know them. When you have an opportunity, recruit them.

2. When you have a critical opening and no viable candidate, use a recruiter and give the recruiter a list of 20 industries comparable to your own. Exceptional people can do exceptional things in many fields. Spend at least several hours with the recruiter. The recruiter will spend weeks and months saving you time, so make the recruiter's time count. Ask for a list of companies the recruiter has recently worked for and therefore cannot recruit out of.

3. Pay the recruiter extra to run some ads. Most choose not to unless you do this. Some good folks respond to ads. Be detailed in the ads in order to naturally start the weeding-out process.

CHAPTER 12

Interview Smarter

"Does he have to know printing?" asked the recruiter.

I answered, "We prefer not. We have too many people that already do." After all, we were a big printing business — Graphic Arts Center of Portland, Oregon.

Graphic Arts Center was the biggest part of U.S. Press, which grew out of Franklin Press, cited in Chapter 11. At the point of this story, Graphic Arts Center was the largest commercial printing business in the western United States.

The recruiter was there because Graphic Arts Center, which had 500 employees, needed a new controller. The recruiter and I talked about what type of controller we should hire. "Get someone who can manage eight people," I said. "Get someone who speaks well, is a CPA, and works hard. He or she must be able to communicate with nonaccountants. He or she should understand accounting is a service function to guide the business, it is not the business itself. But the person must also not let the areas and jobs that are hurting the numbers go unchallenged."

WE HAD THOUGHT a long time about this. There were four of us who would make the final decision, and we all spent time with the recruiter. I was the CEO. The other three were Gayland in Finance, Frank in Production and Don in sales. We knew what we wanted and were in basic agreement. Now it was my turn to talk to the recruiter.

"We need someone who has the courage to ask a few dumb questions about printing because the answers are sometimes dumber than the questions," I said. "It would be great if they came from a job-shop environment. That's what this is; we still spend more time on individual job-cost analysis than we do on the overall profit and loss. I'd like someone with manufacturing experience, in a job shop at least once. Also, get someone from a similiar-sized business."

"Housing and steel fabrication might be good to pick through," suggested the recruiter.

"Bingo and bingo."

We talked about pay and profit bonuses and then I summarized. "A boozer won't work. Can't be too slick or too dull, we're a down-the-middle group in that way, same for aggression. There's a lot of interplay and this person must stand his or her ground without trying to dominate."

In four weeks, the recruiter had ten résumés in my hands. By phone, I cut it to six. We did background checks through Equifax Employment Services. One of the six wasn't paying his bills; another overstated her previous job. Neither seemed like sterling qualities for handling money. The other four checked out, so we brought them in for interviews.

All four candidates came to Graphic Arts Center on the same day and all were paid $500 to write a report about their impressions and suggestions. They were each interviewed by all four of us — Gayland, Frank, Don, and myself. Not a group interview. One at a time, with each of us. Meanwhile, each of us saw a different candidate, one at a time. They didn't see each other and we didn't talk to each other until all the interviews were over. It was bang, bang — one after another after another, and intense. But it eliminated the proven tendency to favor the last interview since each of us talked to a different candidate last. It also eliminated the prejudicial comments that one interviewer hears from another before even seeing a candidate.

THE STRATEGY WAS sound. But Don, in sales, was having a bad day. The computer had broken down, and one of his salesmen had just botched an account. He was unhappy, and it showed in the interviews with all four candidates. But he had a bad day with each equally, thanks to the technique of same-day interviews.

We asked open-ended questions. We hoped for glimpses of the inner person.

For the rest of us who were interviewing, the day got better as it went on — the questions became more pointed with practice. The entire thing boiled down to compatible values, as it always does. We asked open-ended questions. "What's best about your job?" we asked. "Worst? When were you last angry? Why? What's your biggest fear about this job? What do you do in your spare time?" We hoped for glimpses of the inner person.

One guy's name was Bill Pattison. He had nervous energy, a quick laugh, and a sharp mind. More than once, I found myself enjoying his honesty. He was technically astute. Pattison was hired as controller, did a superb job, and remains at the helm today, nine years later.

It was a good hire because it was a sound interview. By interviewing all at once, comparisons were fresh. We knew how each of the candidates thought, and they weren't at the mercy of our mood of the day since each encountered essentially the same mood.

The most incisive of the candidates caused quite a bit

of discomfort with several of the managers. Another was almost as sharp and clearly had better communication skills. Bill Pattison was the best of the lot for this position, and we figured it out the right way. We had few doubts at the end of the day, no doubts when we received their reports.

In his report, Pattison talked about friction in sales and the things that probably had to happen on both sides to stop it. Good, gutsy stuff — quite a contrast to the other candidates. Two wanted to please everybody to get the job, while the third talked about the need to upgrade the computer system as a top priority. We didn't agree.

Only Pattison understood that people were the top priority. He understood what it is to be on a team.

You'll get a stronger crew if you:

1. Do all final interviews in one day. It is tough to get everyone's schedules to match. But no other task is more important.

2. Don't talk too much; ask open-ended questions. Pay attention to the candidates' questions. Remember who asks the best.

3. Check each candidates' background through Equifax Employment Services. They will verify degrees claimed, credit, criminal record, job history, and references. This service costs between $25 and $300, depending on what you need to know. It is well worth it. It gives peace of mind. Also, pay each candidate to give you written suggestions for your business. It is a sample of their work, and you just may learn something.

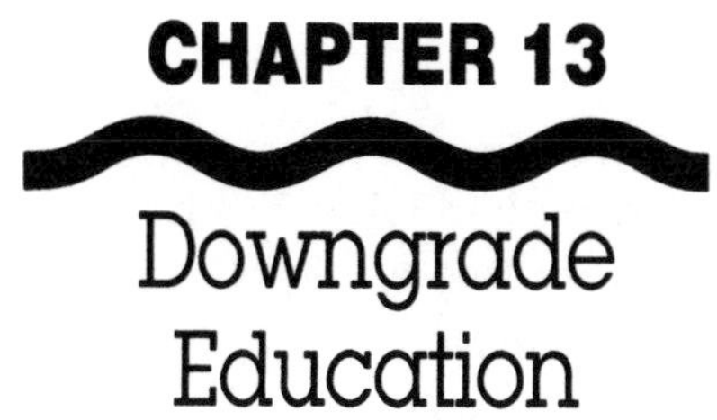

CHAPTER 13

Downgrade Education

Linda Billings had unusual cheer. She was recruited years earlier from Wells Fargo Bank, where she handled Montron's checking account along with 1,000 other clients. She came into accounting at Montron and later became controller, overseeing growth rates of more than 100 percent per year. Then Fisher-Price Toys bought Montron, and Linda became materials manager.

Linda's job was to run warehousing, distribution, purchasing, and production. That's all — just about everything inside.

Her biggest challenge was to install the MRP (Material Requirement Planning) system in the factory. To do this, she needed the cooperation of all her workers. Cooperation and dedication. She needed timely, accurate reports on all sorts of manufacturing data and then she entered those numbers into a computer program that automatically ordered parts based on projected lead times. It was a tricky system to coordinate, but when it worked it made factories hum and inventory fly.

This is no small task. She coordinated scrap rates, engineering changes, and the best-priced ordering quantities. Her style was straightforward. I remember one time watching her against the backdrop of a sunset as she demonstrated to a worker why it shouldn't take two weeks to clean up a pile of pallets. The worker tried to explain why they (the pallets) and he were both sitting idly for two weeks. "I was gonna get to those any minute," he protested.

"Little late," said Linda. She carried a pallet over her head and threw it into the dumpster. All I could see was her silhouette. In fact, that's all I could see of the other worker too. A silhouette. It felt like back row seating in a small theater. Dramatic lighting, dramatic action.

The worker stood frozen in place. Linda walked to the pile and hoisted another pallet. "Do you think I enjoy doing your work for you?" she asked.

HER ARSENAL included more than one method of motivating people. Although she could be hard — tossing wooden pallets — she could also use a soft touch, or more often, polite logic. She had a smile that could melt icebergs. She asked lots of questions and rarely gave orders, although when she did she was commanding.

She was a leader and a manager, always striving for agreement, commitment, and vision. It was a kick to watch her stop a production manager in his tracks and change his direction after just a few words. Inevitably, the production manager would nod and smile and then head off in a new direction with a different priority. I never knew what she said those times. But it worked.

The only certainty between two candidates is that the more educated one will be less excited by the offer.

She had a special touch. When she was first putting

the MRP system in place, she brought a withdrawn and intellectual engineer onto her side. When she first went to him, he kept to himself almost as if he were bound to his drawing board. At lunch, he used to go out to his parked car to nap. He was intelligent but hardly gregarious. He was a loner.

But she needed him for the system to work. She was honest and explained that his support would show the system could work. He was sold on it. It was a metamorphis. Suddenly, he became extroverted, walking into everybody's offices all day long to make sure they were all getting their part done. He was so enthusiastic that everyone tried to stay a step ahead to avoid disappointing him. He was a champion during the setup of the system, and his follow-up with other departments probably saved 30 days in the setup process.

Linda Billings was able to enhance manufacturing efficiency during a period of rapid growth. She coordinated everyone who worked for her, and she nurtured a team atmosphere by doing little things, like buying pizza and soda every day after work for a month. This allowed for an informal review session that was friendly, honest, and incredibly helpful.

LINDA DOES NOT have a college degree. In most companies, this would have prevented her from rising up to the position of authority for which she was so greatly gifted.

It's sad because one legal way to discriminate is to require a degree. The truth is that limiting the number of candidates this way isn't usually very bright. The only certainty between two candidates is that the more educated one will be less excited by the offer.

The rules are, there are no rules. Keep an open mind and see what you can find. Education as a success factor is highly overrated. Intelligence and drive are much more important; compatible values are critical.

Education is fun, once in a while it is even relevant, but your employees need only be smart and motivated.

Your crew will know more than textbook sailing if you:

1. Drop the educational requirements by one notch for every job outside of research and development. Spend more time interviewing a larger group of candidates and pick talent and proven results over degrees.

2. Cut your seminar and training budget in half. Seminars give managers an excuse to delegate training that they should do themselves. Worse, it is delegated to an expensive outsider. Pick one — the expensive outsider or the manager. You don't need both.

3. Always pay for employees to take job-related classes on their own time. Cover all tuition for an A grade, half for a B, and nothing for anything else.

CHAPTER 14

Reverse Discriminate

It was a gritty September day in Tijuana, Mexico, and I had a flat tire. The thermometer swelled mercury red and my own temperature was even hotter because I was on my way to a one-story adobe factory in the warehouse district of town. This had been a bad month. It figured that I was due for a flat.

A month earlier, AFI de Mexico hired 200 new workers. Finding workers was no problem. Applicants lined up thirty rows deep at the front door starting at five every morning. This went on for two weeks.

Despite the overflow of applicants, it was tough. This was a different culture, and I wasn't part of it. There were things I didn't expect. Some of it was interesting. Some of it was sad. We had to teach some new employees, mostly young women, how to use toilet paper in our bathrooms. They had never encountered it before. As a result of poor hygiene, some of them carried tuberculosis or even illnesses less imaginable, like mange.

As we worked our way through the medical problems, we found out the doctor giving the physicals to the new hires was molesting the women. We dealt with it by complaining to the government. Nothing happened to the doctor but at least he stopped molesting our employees.

AFI de MEXICO was six years old, the brainchild of luck and effort described in Chapter 30. Three of our toys became best sellers for Fisher-Price. Those items were a movie viewer, tape recorder, and record player, and they still sell more than two million units a year. In fact, in 1978 when I was running the factory, three of the top ten sellers for Fisher-Price were those of AFI de Mexico. Altogether, Fisher-Price then sold 140 items.

We were incredibly busy that month, running two 56-hour production shifts a week. It just made the sweat run faster and there seemed no stop to it that dusty morning. Two days before, I thought we had reached the low point when dozens of our workers suffered an outbreak of food poisoning from the cart vendors outside our plant. But no, there was more.

On my way to work, I ran over a tumbleweed and got a flat tire. I stood outside in the dust and heat and changed that tire and thought in frustration that maybe some other changes ought to be made.

I couldn't do anything about the medical or molesting problems that wasn't already done, but I had other problems — in production. The setup at AFI de Mexico was that the production line for most items was almost entirely female, yet the Latin machismo culture we borrowed put men on as supervisors. The women worked hard but the men were above it all.

The male supervisors were often standing around gabbing, talking up their weekends at jai alai or whatever. They weren't supervising. They weren't paying attention. They were men, they were above that. That was work.

Yeah, right. The truth is that I put up with it because I assumed it was the culture and nothing could be done.

BUT THERE WAS somebody who thought something should be done. It was one of the women on the production line. Her name was Celia and she caught my attention as soon as I arrived at the factory after changing my tire.

"Señor Sutton," she shrieked, "la liñea esta debajo. Sin partes. Siempre!" The production line was without parts. Again!

We terminated the male supervisors and promoted females to replace them. Production per labor hour went up by about 20 percent within thirty days.

Pablo and Jorge stood by themselves. They didn't see me walk in and they were pointing and laughing, telling stories with chest-thrusting theatrics. I walked to the folder with the production records. Pablo and Jorge had failed to record production rates for the past two hours. Celia told me we had only three boxes of springs left and we had run out of labels a half hour earlier.

That was it. I had thought about getting rid of this layer of arrogance many times before; now there was nothing to lose. I fired Pablo and Jorge and promoted Celia. But I didn't stop there. I fired fourteen of seventeen male supervisors. Invariably, they were the same — a combination plate of macho and lazy.

It wasn't so much the laziness as the strutting. They were so above it all that they didn't care about details. So, with plenty of severance, we terminated the male supervisors and promoted females to replace them.

Life became a cakewalk. Production per labor hour went up by about 20 percent within thirty days. Problems seemed to get caught about a decade earlier and were usually easier, certainly with less pain. There was harmony, production, and happiness.

More often than not, females outproduce males, Orientals beat Caucasians, and youth beat out their elders if they are supervised. Take advantage of it.

Here's how to fill your boat with a more productive crew:

1. Inject new energy into your business by making it resemble your marketplace or neighborhood. There are productive ethnic groups, and they often work harder. Do things differently and watch your company thrive. Hire a female truck driver, a male secretary, or a 70-year-old sales rep.

2. If the new hires don't cut it, replace them as you would anybody.

3. When there's a productive ethnic or cultural group nearby, hire them in batches. They'll police each other. Move one of them into management and let that culture work for you.

CHAPTER 15

Raise Pay, Cut Benefits

In the late 1980s, Dave Cohen opened his second Greentree Foods, a health-food store in New Hampshire. In many ways, it was similiar to his first store.

They both carried sprouts and roots and herbs and dried-fruit-and-nut mixes. Both stores had 2,000-square-foot layouts in well-traveled strip malls, and both were staffed by wholesome granola kids.

But at the first store, Cohen noticed that his clerks stayed only an average of six months. Sure, he was dealing with young employees, and, yes, his clerks stayed twice as long as employees do on average at a fast-food place. But that was small consolation.

Every year, he had to spend chunks of money and time training people and worrying whether they were offending customers because they didn't quite know where the organic ketchup was or what to do with the biodegradable paper cups. And every time there was a new hire, he had to spend the first few days worrying whether the new hire would work out or would show up for a second week.

SO WHEN HE opened his new store, he tried something radically different. He raised the pay and eliminated all the benefits of clerks at the second store.

Here's how it worked: New clerks at the original store made $8 per hour. If they worked 48 hours a week, they made $18,768 a year, including overtime. Plus they got medical coverage, ten paid holidays, and a week of paid vacation during the first year.

At the second store, clerks received nothing but money. No benefits, no vacation, no sick days. Only more money. They were paid $10.40 an hour. If a new clerk at the second store took as many days off — ten holidays, a week of vacation — as a new clerk at the original store, the clerk at the second store made $24,211.

The clerks at the new Greentree Foods have more freedom. When employees worked more, they made more. They took time off when they wanted, and they made $5,443 extra a year. No, they don't have medical insurance, but that $5,443 should pay for equivalent health care and leave some extra. Employees win, employers win.

> Without benefits and the rules they require, the job started to fit the individual, instead of vice versa.

At the new store, clerks stayed more than twice as long. Things were sharper on the floor as customers found things quicker and got better advice.

There was no increase in cost. Even though salaries were 30 percent higher, that was offset by savings from insurance and vacation and sick pay. And there were no costs for administering those programs. The employees were happy to receive the money up front and there was no clamor for benefits or change. It worked better.

There was a college coed at the new store who dropped

back to twenty-five hours and relied on a group policy purchased through school for medical benefits. She took a three-month vacation to go home every summer, and her job was waiting every year when she went back. She made $9,000 during the school year and another $3,500 at another job every summer. This helped put her through school and allowed her to visit home every summer.

Others went to longer hours. One took a two-week vacation every three months. Without benefits and the rules they require, the job started to fit the individual, instead of vice versa. That's nirvana.

Here's how to liberate your crew with better pay and fewer fringes:

1. Form an employee committee to help you plan a dramatic pay increase coupled with a drop in benefits. Announce, one year in advance, an across-the-board pay increase of 20 percent. Also announce a canceling of health benefits, seniority rights, sick days, and paid vacations. (Use the savings to prepay health policies for those few who may be uninsurable.)

2. An alternative is to offer a bonus of $750 per year to employees who will drop their health insurance and show proof they are insured by a working spouse. It will cut the health expense by $1,500 per participant per year — the company saves $750; the employee pockets $750. Every year. Minimum.

3. Give the same benefits immediately to new hires as to twenty-year veterans. All pay and vacation and pension fringes should depend on performance, not on how long they've been breathing company air. If you overpay long-term employees, you shortchange new blood. And that's not how you build a strong company.

CHAPTER 16

Use Some Incentives

In 1976 sales were flat at Checks To–Go, and the attitude of the telemarketers was even flatter. It was a job, they did it, and they left. They essentially responded to the way they were treated. It was understandable, but it was costly.

The telemarketers were paid straight salaries, and poor performance was terminated. There was no recognition given to top performers out of fear they would want more money or become difficult to manage. The only incentives were negative incentives, sort of like spanking a two-year-old. Their supervisor had no use for anything but scare tactics. This guy always came in through the back door so the telemarketers couldn't see him coming. He loved to do that and then just watch. He would pick up a phone log book and stare accusingly at it without establishing eye contact with anyone. When he finished his inquisition into the log books, he would toss them on the desk with a condescending roll of his eyes and then move onto the next employee. He was brutal. Always, he was asking, "How many calls have you made? Why not? What's wrong with you?" He was aching for a personality transplant.

IT WAS OBVIOUS that there was no reason for these people to strive to succeed, so we gave them reason. The first thing we did was replace the old supervisor with a woman who knew something about people and sales. Instead of threatening to fire employees every other day, the new supervisor showed an interest in them and their opinions and perspectives. "What are your customers saying?" she asked. "What can we do to make it better?" She knew that those in the trenches understood the business better than anyone. So she listened.

But there was more. We cut their pay. It was a significant cut — from $10 per hour to $8 — but we also gave them back 1 percent of their sales. The new system meant that even if sales were merely flat, at an average of $2,000 a day, it was a modest raise. But sales weren't flat. Suddenly, the telemarketers had reason to try harder. It was a modest raise, but it was a raise and they earned it. The modest raise created an immodest sales boost of 25 percent.

The new sales manager created weekly contests. When envelopes became overstocked, the person with the most envelope sales that week was given a weekend in Catalina. When things slowed down, whoever created the highest average order size received theater tickets. Everyone was always thinking about success rather than worrying about failure.

> The truth about incentives is that the first dollar you pay is the most effective.

Sales growth and customer satisfaction reflected the new attitude that came from the incentives. They weren't just monetary incentives either. Once, we gave the group a complaint-reduction goal and when they met it, I cooked everyone a lobster dinner at my home. Life became fun for the telemarketers until two years later when Western Certificate acquired Checks To-Go. One of the first things the new owners did was eliminate the incentives, and that's one reason the entire business vaporized within eighteen months of the acquisition.

The thing about incentives is they have to be handled delicately. Several years after installing them at Checks To-Go, I ran Knight Protective Industries (I still do).

Sales at Knight were flat and declining so I thought I knew the cure. The company had 80 telemarketers on the payroll, each making 250 calls per shift. It seemed to me there was a simple solution so I trimmed the base salary by $2 per hour and increased incentives enough to guarantee they would at least break even with identical performance. Déjà vu.

It cratered.

The problem was that Knight telemarketers already had an incentive, with daily bonuses on top of them. More incentives made the top performers wealthier on the same effort but it hurt the average performers, the ones we were trying to motivate.

By then it was too late. We tried to go backward, prior program's where the incentives were more moderate but all that did was make the star sales people disgruntled. They jumped ship. (This is an accomplishment that may never make it to my résumé.)

The truth about incentives is that the first dollar you pay is the most effective. A little incentive always works. Incentives also work best when they remain subservient to teamwork. Positive feedback helps, but helps most when combined with incentives. Motivation should be an overall strategy. Too much incentive fosters greed.

Here's how to "incentivize" your ship overnight:

1. Publicly recognize one employee for outstanding work every month. Reserve a parking place near the door

for that employee, almost as close as the customers' spots. Put the person's picture in the company newsletter with a story about his or her particular customer-service act, cost savings, or production.

2. Make at least 5 percent of every employee's pay a monthly bonus for his or her department's specific goals (that is, number of error-free transactions in accounting without overtime, units shipped minus 100 for every return in production, days outstanding in collection, beating budget and schedule in research, and so forth.) Tie these bonuses to groups of 20 or fewer individuals to develop peer pressure and teamwork. Don't create lone wolves with individual bonuses unless a task is clearly a solo effort. Then do it big.

3. Post department goals in each area on bar charts or graphs that can be read from 30 feet away. Make these the center of attraction in all tours and walks through the offices. Always stop, look, comment, and discuss.

CHAPTER 17

Tighten the Ship

In the spring of 1988, Western Certificate acquired Checks To-Go. I was president of Checks To-Go. Both companies produced bank checks. Western printed for banks in huge quantities. Their buyers were sophisticated, placing huge daily orders.

Checks To-Go created checks for small PC users. We bought checks in bulk and then personalized them for the customers. But our customers often didn't know their account number, how many to order, what type of forms they needed, and how to load them in their printer. They ordered only once or twice a year. They needed our help.

When the transaction was complete, I ran the new division. I worked for Western Certificate. Up to that moment, Checks To-Go made the highest profits of any company in the check industry. Western bought us because it wanted to enter the growing PC business. Western entered at the top.

IN THE FIRST meeting in their board room in Denver, when I officially became part of what they called "the 'A' team," we talked first about — no, not checks. Not customers. We talked about hotels. They didn't like the one I was staying in. They were uncomfortable that I was a Priority Club member at Holiday Inn.

The executive vice-president smiled and explained. "We prefer someone of your level to stay at the Marriott or Hilton. We need to keep up an image."

This guy was splendid in his French cuffs, monograms, and braided red suspenders. Never bet on a guy wearing designer suspenders to understand cost controls. Or to want to.

I knew that a night at the Denver Marriott or Hilton ran about $80. Holiday Inn was running about $50. Their choices cost about 60 percent more.

All had clean beds and a bathroom. Breakfast too. I thought of this as the executive vice-president continued. "You are now part of a new team. We need consistency in the organization, so you should stay with the Marriott in Denver and its equivalent elsewhere." He expected I'd be eager to join this upscale group.

Image ruled. They changed their name from Western Certificate to Wescert because they were expanding beyond the region. They asked my opinion of the switch and I said, "It has all the charm of International House Of Pancakes calling itself IHOP."

Never bet on a guy wearing designer suspenders to understand cost controls.

They also asked me what kind of car I wanted. I had a choice of an Oldsmobile Cutlass or a Mercury Sable.

I told them I didn't want a car.

THEY FIRED ME six weeks later for disagreeing with their business strategy. They viewed Checks To-Go as a production business, needing economies of scale. This reflected their primary business.

I viewed it as a service business.

So I left the company for medical reasons. They were sick of me.

In eighteen months, Checks To-Go was gone. Kaput. They disappeared. They could no longer print checks. They couldn't write on them — they couldn't pay their own bills. Somehow, $3 million had disappeared.

Nice image, eh?

Look, there are few companies in America that make as much as 10 percent profit on sales. Most make about 3 percent to 4 percent. With that tiny margin, everything counts, especially a chance at 60 percent in savings.

And remember, the Marriott is not just the Marriott. The Marriott is like one small hole in your corporate ship, but its mere existence leads to pressure for other holes to spurt. Need new equipment? *Who cares, go for it now.* And then another leak — *fancy new offices to keep up the image.* Pretty soon water is gushing in. And then the iceberg, *a recession.*

Heavy ships sink faster. Uncontrolled costs destroy any business, and limos and Marriotts and luxury are uncontrolled costs. If your competitor has a limo and you don't, you are already winning. He has a leak.

There have been five self-made multibillionaires (say that five times fast, just for fun) in the United States in recent years. Sam Walton founded Walmart. In 1991, he drove an eight-year-old red Ford pickup. He always fetched his own coffee. One time, when a friend of mine was in the Walmart lobby, he watched as Walton accidentally spilled his coffee out of the machine, grabbed some paper towels, and mopped it up himself.

Ross Perot paid himself $70,000 a year as president of Electronic Data Systems — EDS. When Perot sold EDS to General Motors, the president of General Motors, Perot's new boss, made a $2.4 million salary plus a bonus. Finally, he paid Perot $2.5 billion to go away because GM executives were embarrassed by the folksy Perot, who didn't want a big salary or office or specially tuned cars. Worse yet, Perot invited employees home to dinner and talked with them constantly. The president of General Motors recently announced layoffs of 72,000.

David Packard never had an enclosed office before he left Hewlett Packard for government service. It figures.

That is three out of the five self-made multibillionaires of the 1980s. The other two, Bill Gates of Microsoft and John Kluge of Metromedia, are spenders, but they haven't been around as long either.

Here's how every business "ship" can be tightened:

1. Downgrade hotels one level. Your customers stay at the Holiday Inn and your competitors are at the Marriott. Whom do you want to know? The bus gets downtown from the airport just as fast as most cabs. Get rid of the company plane. Commercial flights get you there quicker, they are safer, and they don't isolate you from other people, some of whom may be your customers.

2. Stop building and equipping new offices. If somebody absolutely has to have an assistant, let him or her share a desk and space. (Watch this cut requests for new hires.)

3. Do little things: reuse paper on the back side; shut off the lights; cut express mail costs by using economy when possible. Withstand the jibes and ridicule for "counting paper clips" and keep it up until the attitude spreads. Don't spend a lot of time on these items. Do them quickly and quietly, then refocus on the bigger picture.

CHAPTER 18

Publish a Firing Policy

For six months in 1974, business at the Broadway Bowl in Littleton, Colorado, doubled. The alleys themselves weren't so busy but every day between 4:30 and 5:30 P.M. there was a huge gathering of engineers with pocket protectors, marketing guys in tassled loafers, and production supervisors in short sleeves and clip–on ties draped all over the bar. The number of daily kegs at the bar jumped from four to eight.

The Broadway Bowl was at 5499 South Broadway. Next door, at 5501 South Broadway, sat Honeywell, and there was clearly a panic. These were less gatherings than therapy sessions. Thirty seconds from Honeywell's front door was enough hops and barley to help all of us deal with the uncertainty.

FOR MORE THAN ten years, Honeywell had distributed the popular line of Pentax cameras in the United States. We operated out of an old supermarket that had been converted into offices and warehouse space.

For a while, that was the way of the Japanese camera market. But Minolta dropped their U.S. distributor two years earlier and Canon canceled their distribution contract with Bell and Howell seven months after Minolta's action. The strategy was to become more aggressive in the United

States. By forgoing profits and pumping more money into advertising and price cuts, they hoped to capture and dominate sales in America.

This was the changed atmosphere that Pentax faced in 1974, a year before their distribution contract with Honeywell expired.

The strategy was a tax strategy as well as one of growth. The change meant that Canon and Minolta would realize profits only in Japan, thus eliminating taxes in the United States. It was a sound, if unfair, strategy, and we at Honeywell knew it. Sales at both Canon and Minolta jumped, and we started going more and more to the Broadway Bowl.

If Honeywell were to follow the example of the competitors — more advertising and price cuts — the obvious outcome was less profits and more sales. And Honeywell didn't have the Japanese market to support it.

CLEARLY, SOMETHING had to give. Pentax wanted more sales in the United States, while Honeywell artfully dug in its heels. Honeywell wanted profits so it continued with modest advertising and what seemed to be fair prices. Pentax balked.

In this particular division of Honeywell, almost all the profits came from Pentax. Pentax wanted more sales than Honeywell could afford so Pentax threatened to follow the lead of the others — Canon and Minolta. Pentax refused to renew Honeywell's distribution contract.

Firing is about what a company stands for.

The question was: Are they bluffing? The truth was, losing Pentax probably meant that this division of Honeywell would go out of business.

Every employee knew this, and we were all uptight. The favored way to vent our collective spleens was to hit the Broadway Bowl and down a few pitchers of Coors. We all knew the problems. There was nothing we could do, because maybe they were bluffing for better terms on the next contract. It wouldn't have been the first time in history. The other question was if Pentax were really going to drop Honeywell, whether they would hire most of the current employees or whether they would start a new company with entirely new employees.

Coors went down real easy. There was too much pressure and not enough answers.

AND THEN ONE day K. Chiwata showed up. He was Pentax's export director, a Japanese who spoke five other languages. We never knew anyone quite like him. He showed up in a loud plaid sportcoat and a mastery of English slang that made him seem more like one of us than us. He absorbed alcohol in mythical quantities and remained coherent, happy, and confident.

We went to dinner with Chiwata and he brought predictable but bad news from Japan. Pentax wanted to control their own distribution and the cancellation was no bluff. Chiwata announced that Pentax would drop Honeywell in one year when the current contract expired. They would start their own distribution, using many Honeywell employees. They would also keep their corporate offices in Denver — a huge relief. Most jobs were safe.

"We could have been friends for many years, and I hope this planned change does not upset you too much," Chiwata said that day. "We will take over and manage the distribution as Pentax Corporation next year," he said.

"I will move from Hong Kong to Denver and we will set up a new distribution center ten minutes from here in the tech center. And I promise we will have fun. All of you will be kept on the payroll. The way we will do it is to guarantee all jobs and pay for the first six months. After that, some positions will disappear, and I have no idea how many or which ones. If you stay through the first six months and your job is eliminated, we will give you six more months' pay as severance. If your job is kept, you will make at least as much and probably more, but you may have more duties. If you quit before the first six months, you get nothing."

Finally, it was clear. Even though it was also murky, the deal was on the table, and it was more than fair. Suddenly, we all stopped worrying about the economy and instead began, again, concentrating on our jobs. We didn't worry about what the government or competition or other outsiders might do to hurt the business. Nervous speculation ceased and an unheard-of thing happened: People took care of their own responsiblities. They took good care.

Smiles returned. Productivity soared, and errors dropped. Few workers wanted their position eliminated but at least there was nothing to worry about for six months, and those dismissed would be cushioned with cash. Life went on, and plans could be made for the future.

The only problem was at the Broadway Bowl, where beer sales dropped as dramatically as they had risen. We all went back to work. Worrying was useless. Mr. Chiwata had laid it all out for us.

It wasn't exactly a hiring policy, but it sort of was a firing policy. We knew where we stood. And that's the point.

Most companies have hiring policies. Few have firing policies. Hiring is a pleasant process and has been analyzed in detail. Firing is more important. It establishes a company's soul. Firing is about what a company stands for. It's easy to have a hiring policy, since hiring is a positive move, yet firing is more controversial and therefore should be better understood. It's time to eliminate paranoia.

Here's how to get the whole crew rowing again:

1. In practice, give specific written warnings for habitual problems before terminating. Employees should be given a chance to respond and correct the problem or challenge the complaint. Policy violations or dishonest behavior should not need such a warning. If a firing is a surprise, management failed.

2. Accrue severance for all employees as a liability in the range of two weeks for every year's service. This means that when a layoff is necessary, some earnings have been set aside to ease the blow for employees and the employer. There's less temptation to be cheap and dishonorable when a recession or sales slump tempts you to scrimp on severance. Accounting practice guides a company to do the opposite under the theory that all businesses are ongoing. The assumption is wrong, so the practice is wrong.

3. Make it clear in the employee manual that employees are free to quit anytime with a two-week notice. Also make it clear that any employee can be fired for any reason at any time. This is at odds with real practice, as previously stated, but is an example of how excessive laws create hypocritical actions. There is no alternative. This is not a nice thing to say, but it must be stated publicly to legally protect your company. For those rare positions where there is a job contract, put a clause in for binding arbitration to settle disputes. Litigation can be an unfair hardship on the employee, and it takes too long. A jury verdict can destroy an employer. Arbitration is best.

CHAPTER 19

Beat the Union

Frederick was the executive vice-president of Checker Press. It was ironic because he was a thirty-year union member who had joined management eight years earlier. He didn't care about production. He didn't care about the union either. The guy was shy.

One year, Frederick was the management negotiator at a contract negotiation, and I was the "headquarters guy" who stopped by one day a month. I tried my best to stay on the sidelines and watch. That day I did.

I was flabbergasted by the first words from the employee representative. They were tragic. "I don't even know you," he said. He was talking to Frederick.

IT WAS TRUE. They had never talked. This was a small company of about 100 employees, and the manager had never even spoken with this particular employee. It was astounding, and it was apparent to the employee that if the manager had never spoken to him, the employee representative, he had probably never spoken to a few other regular employees.

Yet there they were, trying to reach, in theory, an amicable agreement on numerous matters of supreme importance to both sides. They shook hands, but it was obviously, and tragically, an impersonal negotiation.

It's not as if there weren't chances before the negotiation for things to be better. It's just that the manager never took advantage of the opportunities. Instead, he chose to be reclusive. He was a steady worker, focused and dedicated. But he never used the most essential of management skills — getting to know his people.

And now he would pay the price: irrational demands that destroyed his business.

The problem was that he didn't relate well and didn't seem to want to relate. And so, it was obvious that although the negotiation turned sour at the negotiating table, the real battle was lost months earlier at the company picnic. It was lost every day in the lunchroom, in the halls, wherever the manager walked and averted his eyes from direct contact with those he led. He may have been bashful but the employees didn't take it that way. They took him to be aloof.

THE PROBLEM with unions isn't with the unions or the employees, it is with management. Always has been. The problem is self-created by lazy, disinterested, and sometimes unfair management. Mismanagement creates unions.

But it doesn't stop there. There is a reason to beat the unions and that is that once the mistrust takes hold, it snowballs. Unions are adversarial by nature. Without conflict, union officials are out of work.

Mismanagement creates unions.

We saw it at Checker Press, two years after the aforementioned negotiation. I was CEO of the parent holding company by then, and I was invited to sit in and observe what my managers told me would be "an interesting spectacle."

There were seven of us around a yellow Formica table.

It was an instant-coffee moment. Two were from management, two were outside union representatives. The other two were the shop steward and the guest of honor — a platemaker who had been fired and was filing a grievance.

It went on for three grueling hours. I tried my best not to get involved. After all, it wasn't really my fight. But I couldn't resist when one of the union representatives repeatedly claimed Checker Press unfairly dismissed the worker.

"Wait a minute," I blurted out, "this guy was caught stealing. He was caught red-handed, caught in fact by other union workers. Not only was he stealing our materials but he also set up a competing business outside." I stopped and sipped some rancid coffee. "And he's been using nonunion labor to undercut our prices and cost your union jobs. You call that an unjust firing? I've got an idea. How about if we go to the newspapers with this unjust firing. I can see the headline now: 'Union Leaders Defend Stealing and Scab Shop.'"

"No newspapers," said the union representative. He scratched his chin. "Look, we don't care about all that. You abused this worker's rights. It is our sacred bond to protect him."

Sacred bond? Hmmm. Well, the meetings went on for two weeks. Finally, the union came to understand the firing was justified. But the union won part of the grievance, too. The termination was handled wrongly, without arbitration or a hearing. I guess the union realized that everything they heard in the grievance would have come out in arbitration. The problem was all the wasted time debating a matter that wasn't debatable. The guy was stealing. Case closed.

Here's what else happened during those two weeks. The strongest local competitor, a nonunion shop, snatched away two major jobs because we were too busy dealing with this problem to dedicate time to the customers. And all the workers at the competitor didn't pay union dues, so they made more money than those at Checker Press.

There is only one way to beat the union — earn the trust of employees. That's the game. It's about being real. If you win the trust game, your company can win in the market. If you lose, you are set up in an adversarial situation that will only drain energy.

Here's how to get the crew all rowing in the same direction:

1. Set up a 401(K) retirement plan that is better than any union fund. It's easy. Every 401(K) is better than every union plan, because workers keep it whether they stay at the same shop or not. When a 401(K) is set up in a union shop, it should be offered to all — union and nonunion. Many union workers will see the benefit and leave the union plan. They must continue to pay dues, though, and they essentially receive nothing in return for those dues. Eventually, half the workers will drop the union, and you can stop recognizing it without a need for a vote with many contracts. Strikes become illegal, and cooperation becomes a reality. Finally.

2. Never hire outside experts to lead your labor negotiations. This should not be a battle. Work is collaboration. Certainly, there needs to be some outside consultation at times, but negotiations are ultimately based on trust, not authoritative bullying or legal trickery.

3. Participate with employees in more than just work. Go bowling, to ball games, picnics, charity work. Play cards together. Don't fake it; that will backfire. It has to be genuine. Mix it up with different departments and different levels. The only way to succeed is to enjoy one another.

CHAPTER 20

Fight Politics

It started as Bill Lear's dream. In the early 1960s, when the Swiss government quit competing with Americans and Soviets in the weapons game, the Swiss cut off funds for a proposed Swiss fighter-bomber. Lear took advantage of the Swiss retreat and bought the designs and tools for the jet from the Swiss government. It was a fire sale. He got it all cheap.

His idea was simple and so was his premise. He would build the world's first private jet based on the idea that there are lots of rich people who would want one or think they need one.

Lear brought all his tools back to Wichita, Kansas, and he established Learjet — a toy for the rich, a tool for the talented. It was truly a jet. If you stood it on its tail it could reach 30,000 feet in five minutes.

Lear had a great idea, but he ran out of money. So he went to Charlie Gates, the owner of Gates Rubber of Denver, who bought a franchise, essentially, to sell Gates Learjets in the United States from Stapleton Airport in Denver. Everything else about Learjet, including production, remained as was in Wichita.

It was a marriage of convenience, but it collapsed $20 million later because of a clash of egos and refusals to share information or cooperate. I know. I was part of it.

Politics is a popular organizational sport, with disinformation, nasty names, and doubt spreading. When you're in it, it seems necessary and sometimes even fun. With the benefit of hindsight, after a collapse, it looks childish and counterproductive.

HERE IS WHAT happened at Lear and Gates Learjet. In 1968, I was hired as manager of public relations for Gates Learjet in Denver. It was a kick. The tough part was mental. I had to sell the idea that Learjets are necessary and efficient tools for a fast crowd of business and government types. First I had to sell myself. It took a while, but I understood. I ski; others fly Learjets. A small difference of cash.

We sold the jets by stretching some assumptions about money and time savings and then putting the stretches into a three-ring binder and calling it a "travel analysis." The assumptions couldn't bear close scrutiny, but they seemed to neutralize bankers and potential shareholder critics. Then I got publicity. I flew with the *Business Week* bureau chief for the Rockies to Wichita for lunch and back in one day. I did a similar trip with a *Fortune* freelancer.

When perception becomes paramount and results irrelevant, it's time to step back and reset priorities.

It was fun and I was filled with all sorts of tidbits for the press, such as how Bill Lear redesigned the leading edge of the wing and then ignored engineering quotes of $200,000 to build it. Instead, he hired a local body-and-fender guy and paid him more than than the guy had ever seen in a year, but Lear still saved well more than $150,000. He also got it done in two days instead of eighteen months. The problem with my tidbits were that they weren't only my tidbits. I had competition.

The problem with my competition was, it was from the same company. I worked for Gates Learjet in Denver. My competition was three other PR flaks for Learjet in Wichita.

It wasn't pretty.

No one was in charge, so we were all in charge. We all put out stories to the press. To the same reporters. And because there was competition among all of us — and, frankly, not nearly enough news to go around — we got creative. Sometimes, we became devious.

We were in the same company, but we rarely talked. Everything was secret. It was obvious when I sent out a press release claiming we sold twenty-two planes the previous year. A reporter from *Fortune* called. He said he had a press release from Wichita claiming only eighteen planes had been sold. "What's the deal?" he asked.

It was a good question. Who knew? Everything was based on orders, but some were firm and some soft, and there were projections for both companies.

We all battled terribly to see who could get the most ink. More press releases meant more chances for contradictions. It was common, and it seemed normal.

Once, heart-transplant surgeon Michael Debakey of Houston wanted to buy a jet. His business manager talked with us in Denver, and he talked to the folks in Wichita. We told him there was no way to put a bathroom in such a small jet. The people in Wichita knew better and told him. Of course, when they worked out the new option a year earlier, they never told us. In fact, when we asked, they told us bathrooms were impossible.

After the bathroom incident, the Wichita people ran to owner Charlie Gates and called me and my Denver colleagues incompetent and claimed they could do a better job by themselves.

WE IN DENVER weren't exactly Boy Scouts. We interfered with production — all done in Wichita — by calling the General Electric factory that made all the engines for the jets. After Wichita had ordered engines based on their forecasts, we guaranteed we could sell an additional twenty engines, and GE made those extra engines.

But sales slumped, as the folks in Wichita suspected could happen. When Wichita tried to slow down deliveries of more engines, they learned that the "Denver dreamers," as they derisively called us, had guaranteed the orders, and they had to take them. One dozen extra engines, at $200,000 per engine, sat around for almost a year before they were needed. Ooops.

Everybody complained about everybody. It was constant, mean-spirited, and counterproductive. Gates Learjet was gone in a few years, a $20 million lesson in the expense of politics and vague responsibilities. Learjet was sold and then finally took off when the new owners did away with politics and instead devoted that competitive energy to develop new models geared to the changing market. What a concept!

Every business faces politics to some degree, and nothing weakens an organization faster than politics overshadowing results. The successful ones know how to deal straight without the games and one-upmanship. When perception becomes paramount and results irrelevant, it's time to step back and reset priorities. Here's how to establish the daily drill for your crew:

1. Pinpoint responsibility for every job. Make goals clearly stated and as measurable as possible, then support every individual in his or her effort to meet these objectives. Encourage teamwork and discourage political games of "Gotcha!"

2. Never set up shadow governments or intercompany spying. Every worker should be responsible for his or her

own work. This reduces the expense and harassment of too many supervisors. Eliminate every position that has the word "assistant," "coordinator," or "liaison" in it. Give them real jobs.

3. When employees complain about other employees, make them do it in the other person's presence. Make sure everybody is hearing the same problem. Don't play Henry Kissinger, jumping from one side to the other. Avoid shuttle diplomacy; force face-to-face talk.

CHAPTER 21

Walk the Floor

David Packard and Bill Hewlett understood a lot more than mere technology when they started their company in Palo Alto, California. They understood people.

It was because of this that they grew their company from a small garage in Packard's backyard into the leader in test instruments, engineering, calculators, medical products, and computers.

Their success became legendary by the early 1980s, and therefore it attracted attention from all corners. Management consultants, business-book writers, and columnists studied Hewlett Packard and all came to essentially the same conclusion.

It was really quite simple; it even had sort of an acronym — MBWA. It was Management By Walking Around — a hands-on management system that stressed listening skills and participation in the day-to-day operation of the entire company. There was no magic to it.

Bill Hewlett kept walking all areas, such as shipping, to see where the river of orders in and orders out was flowing at the time. He learned a lot on the loading docks. Hewlett moved on from shipping when he was satisfied. But he knew he would come back soon.

Next, he would go to production to find out the quirks

of hard-to-solder joints from the workers on the floor Monday and the variability of resistors on Tuesday. Often, he would spend days with production. He always tried to think of how any specific design change would affect all those in production.

BUT HEWLETT was a scientist by trade, and it was there that his philosophy really came through. One Saturday, he stopped to examine some subassemblies and found he needed a microscope. The problem was that all the microscopes were locked up for the weekend. Hewlett was frustrated. This was his company. Those were his microscopes.

But they weren't just his. They belonged to the company. They belonged to anybody in the company qualified to use them. He was qualified.

It was Management By Walking Around — a hands-on management system that stressed listening skills and participation in the day-to-day operation of the entire company.

But the microscopes were locked away, and this made no sense at all, so Hewlett did the only thing he could think of that was logical. He took a crowbar and pried open the lock that closed the chain-link gate over the equipment area. He took his microscope, but before he left that room he wrote a note for the first person in on Monday morning. It said, "Please don't ever lock this equipment again," and it was signed, Bill Hewlett.

Dave Packard had the same commitment to improving the daily operation of the company. He was always looking to improve, trying to learn more about the inner workings. Sometimes, he checked receivables to see if any customers were slowing up. Other times, he went with a new salesman on a cold call — just to get to know the salesman and to keep a feel for the field.

Sales at Hewlett Packard hit $15 billion in 1991. They grew by keeping the hierarchy from growing so big that they lost touch. They kept in touch by walking the floor, and as they grew they made sure the practice of walking the floor was passed down to mid-level management people. They did it for one reason. It worked.

Here's how to keep the feel of the deck:

1. Walk the floor day and night and ask questions. Don't always go at the same time, or even the same shift. The night folks have different concerns and problems and different suggestions. Share the dirty work. Go along on a sales call to Buffalo in January, or to Louisiana in July just to show you're there for business.

2. Get rid of the sign-in book at your front desk. It has no use, except to help visiting salespeople discover their competition. Open the place up, get rid of the paranoia.

3. Visit remote locations instead of communicating by memo. If it's not important enough to visit, it's not important enough to keep. Use as little electronic and paper communication as possible. Talk more, dictate less.

PART 3

SHIP SHAPE: Running Better Internally

CHAPTER 22

Control Debt

Intermark is a holding company in La Jolla, California, traded on the American Stock Exchange. They always borrowed and bought. They had a magic touch. They borrowed to the limit, and they bought more and more.

I was CEO of Franklin Press, a well-run $7 million printing company in dusty San Bernadino (described in Chapter 11). I knew about Intermark because, well, they bought Franklin Press and then hired me to run it.

Intermark promised we would combine Franklin with Arts & Crafts Press if I managed to learn printing. The goal was to eventually find another printer to buy after that and ultimately take the group public in five years. It was my baby, and amazingly, it almost worked. Almost.

IT LOOKED AS IF it was going to work when Intermark was booming in 1983. Intermark owned about a dozen companies and was rolling along when it decided to take a couple of giant steps. It seemed great, only Intermark decided to step in another direction.

I wanted only $3 million cash and another $8 million in notes to acquire Graphic Arts Center. But Intermark first went for different and far bigger acquisitions. They bought a $50-million wheel company. And then there was a huge sporting goods distributor. The next acquisition was Pier One. Suddenly, there was about $300 million in new debt just to pay for these companies.

When I first approached the management of Intermark about Graphic Arts Center, the executive vice-president screamed that it was "crazy." Eventually, I talked them into negotiating and they bought Graphic Arts Center reluctantly, and at a trifle higher price than we could have had we acted with more enthusiasm.

The first year, Graphic Arts Center's profits jumped from $1.5 million to $2.2 million. Profits plummetted the next year so we slashed expenses, and the following year profits passed $3 million. The acquisition was half paid for out of its own cash flow in three years, then sold for $25 million. Intermark did well.

When you play double-or-nothing forever, the result is always the same.

On the other buys, though, Intermark wasn't so lucky. The glamorous acquisitions that they jumped on never came close to paying their way.

In 1992, Intermark entered bankruptcy. It was tragic. On the one hand, anyone who invested $20,000 in 1973 was worth millions in 1983. Of course, ten years after that it was worth about a double cheeseburger and some fries — if you cooked it yourself.

The problem with Intermark was that it took risk taking to an extreme. When you play double-or-nothing forever, the result is always the same. In the steady-growth 1980s it worked. But as soon as the market hiccupped, Intermark was in trouble. They pushed debt too far.

If Intermark had simply stopped buying and borrowing in 1983, it probably would have been a nice little money-maker today. It wouldn't be a billion-dollar mess, it would be a $300 million asset.

Debt is your ultimate fair weather friend. Here's how to keep debt from sinking your boat:

1. Put together a "ten-year flood plan" for every business, much as a city planner does. Guess the worst possible year for your business and then set the debt levels needed to survive that year. Attach the number to every plan you ever do, and never exceed the debt levels it allows. You'll miss a couple of opportunities, but you'll survive the unexpected — which you should expect.
2. Examine your competitors' debt levels when you set yours. If they are slugs, put yours higher and outrun them. If they are leaner and meaner than you, invest internally, cut your debt, and don't butt heads with them as much in the marketplace.
3. Anytime that rates are low and you are tempted to borrow, don't. Take a long walk, shower, and go to a movie. Never borrow money because it is cheap. Borrow only when forced to by overwhelming opportunity.

CHAPTER 23

Dodge Computer Traps

Metaltreet is a subsidiary of the Precision Machine Company of Seattle. Precision Machine is the largest manufacturer of metal parts in the Western United States.

It was January and the slow rain was colder than usual in Seattle. I had become CEO of Precision Machine the day before. As the new CEO, I replaced a thirty-three-year veteran who had slacked off the last two years. It wasn't his company anymore. It was being run by his CFO. It was being run by numbers.

In the previous two years, Precision Machine had grown fast. The company had splurged on equipment. Sales jumped, but debt grew faster.

I was hired because the veteran CEO was fired. His demise came when the economy burped and profits disappeared. When I was hired, I had thirty-three years less experience in metal manufacturing than my predecessor had.

As I started on the job, I saw that people at the company worked hard, but the hard work was misdirected. The hardest worker of all was the CFO. He was a maniac on the mainframe. He was the CFO — he knew his purpose. He created reports.

The day after I took control, I went to visit our subsidiary, Metaltreet. Metaltreet specialized in treating parts after they were made.

The treatment could be heating the parts to relieve internal stresses, deburring sharp edges, or shotpeening the surfaces to eliminate surface irregularities. Pacific Metals did all these for its parent company and other competitors.

I met the general manager, Bill Holiday, in his office. He was friendly and wide open, happy to have some attention. We shook hands and sat down. As I sat, I noticed a stack of computer printouts on his desk. I asked about them. It was innocent. I was just curious.

"Bill, how do you use those reports?" I asked.

He looked at me. He grinned, and then held it back. "I get my paper clips from them" he said.

"I don't get it."

"Watch."

He picked up the report of green-and-white striped computer paper. It was at least a quarter-inch thick. Bill pulled the thick metal clip off the report. He reached into an upper desk drawer and pulled out an oversized coffee cup. He dropped the paper clip into the black cup and put the cup back in the drawer. And then he pushed the report off the edge of the side of his desk. It plopped into the circular file.

Can any economy survive with 20 million people doing spreadsheets?

"I never complain, and they never complain," he said. "I've got a lot of other things to do, and it saves me searching for paper clips." He smiled.

I UNDERSTOOD where he was coming from, but it was

a deception. All of it was, especially the reports. The MIS Department felt good for being so productive in generating reports. Division managers loved them for the paper clips and nothing else, and top management never heard anything about it so they just assumed everything was under control because there was so much information in the reports.

Most of it was useless information. It was information nobody wanted.

This is how we solved the problem: We demoted the MIS head one level. Now, the managers of sales, production, and accounting could shove him around a little. The MIS department became a service department again. It served; it didn't dictate. The problem was overuse of the box.

There are about 12 million owners of the Lotus 1-2-3 spreadsheet software in the United States. There are probably 8 million owners of other spreadsheet software. Can any economy survive with 20 million people doing spreadsheets? That's 20 million people not producing anything to sell.

It used to be that people had to think, they had to act. Back in the dark ages of the 1970s at Honeywell, where I was director of product management, we were arguing about cost versus return on a potential new slide projector. We fought. This would sell better than that, we argued. No, that had a better sales potential, they countered. Passions rose and people stood up for what they believed. Over two prototypes, we stood nose to nose and talked about their respective financial merits.

One group supported building the projector that cost $99 retail and was expected to sell 50,000 units per year. The other group supported the $149 projector that was expected to sell 25,000 units per year.

Why the debate? Because it had to be decided before the bean counters could get to it. There wasn't time to do a bunch of detailed "what-ifs." Once we decided the most likely unit sales for each price and what the most probable cost to produce would be, the accountants took those numbers for two prolonged weeks of manual spreadsheet agony.

Not today. Have you seen a bad pro forma recently? Every manager has a PC. Most have spreadsheets that spit out answers in twenty minutes. If the return looks bad, just change the assumptions: raise sales or lower costs with keyboard magic until the return is acceptable.

The agony is gone. The mental anguish has vanished. That's the problem. The thought process hits a stop sign. *Nobody thinks about the assumptions anymore*. They are created to fit the desired results, and bad products are born.

Here's how to free your vessel of computer tyranny:

1. Simplify. Kill any computer report that isn't dog-eared by the end of the day. At least once a year hold a report-killing meeting and don't let anybody leave until three or four are buried. Ask everyone which reports are used and then ask what actions were taken as a result. Anything that's not read, dies. Anything that is read but doesn't lead to action also dies.

2. Sell your mainframe now. You are not using most of it anymore. You will take a beating on price, but if you don't sell it you will take a far worse beating next year. Get rid of that unused capacity while it can be sold. Let each department buy their PCs if they can justify it. Usually, they can't. Make them produce a hard-nosed cost saving that will result by adding a PC. Don't let it be based on some new activity that "should" greatly improve things. Make it save labor on existing work. If it's close, don't do it. No computer has performed to expectations with less labor than predicted yet in this ice age. Don't let the MIS department "coordinate" PC purchases. Networking never saves enough labor to justify a department or to justify creating overhead by overseeing the network.

3. Cancel any meeting that reviews pro formas or projections. Don't allow group discussions of those numbers. Change the subject to discussions of the assumptions (market, costs, price) that go into the calculations. After a consensus is reached on the assumptions, anybody with a PC can do the pro forma in minutes.

CHAPTER 24

Create Productive Meetings

It was startling. When I first arrived at Checks To-Go, they never had staff meetings. It was great except for one thing, it simply didn't work.

This was too bad because it would be life enhancing to get rid of most meetings, but the problem was nobody made commitments. They guessed.

Production didn't know what sales was hoping to do next month. They guessed.

Accounting didn't know what productions costs were likely to be, and accounting never told sales that the low prices offered were costing profits. Nobody talked and everybody, when necessary, guessed about the other.

What a system.

There was only one thing to do. I called a meeting, and the conversation went something like this:

"We're losing money."

"What do you mean we're losing money? Sales are up 30 percent."

"Big deal. You gave away 15 percent in promotional expense. And not only that. None of that was scheduled so we had to special order Peachtree forms and pay a premium."

What a surprise.

But we kept at it. The first meeting had rough edges when we first sat down and tried to explain our different perspectives. They sure were different, sometimes strained. But we kept at it, one hour at a time.

That's right, we had a one-hour meeting and when it ended it was over, to paraphrase that great business leader, Yogi Berra. And then we held another, and another, once a week for an hour. Finally, after two months of melting acrimony, the managers began to understand teamwork. Why it works. What they need to do, and what they deserve to expect. They realized the purpose of meetings is to find problems and fix them. The purpose was not to blame people, and when everyone realized that, things started to open up.

The purpose of meetings is to find problems and fix them.

Finally, things were different. Finally, there was a conversation that went like this:

"Can we do another promotion for June on the Open Systems forms?"

"We're a little short but if you can push it to the second half of the month, we can get ready for it without needing a special order."

"That's great. If we do a mailing today, bulk rate, we should get some extra business at just the right time without much extra expense."

"We'll be ready."

"We'll do it and see what happens."

What a company. There were profits. In 1984, Checks To-Go was picked by *Inc.* magazine as one of the nation's 500 fastest growing businesses. In 1987, the company had the highest operating profits in the industry.

IN MARCH 1988, Wescert acquired Checks To-Go and reasoned that if one meeting worked so well then a bunch of meetings would work even better. They increased the meeting schedule to sixteen hours a week on every conceivable subject. The scene was wonderful, employees staring at employees while forecasting and reforecasting. They planned and replanned. They talked and talked and talked about work.

See the problem?

They

talked about work; they didn't work! Only about one to two hours of that was productive — the rest was jaw exercises. It's not that there were problems among employees. Everyone got along fine, and in fact, the meetings were fun. The problem was that for essentially two days a week, the managers were all meeting and having social fun while all their work backlogged.

All that planning didn't help because they lost their customer base, and eighteen months after being the profit leader of the industry, Checks To-Go vanished.

Keep the regatta going without overcontrol. Try to:

1. Spend between three and six hours a week in meetings. Three or more people talking is a meeting.

2. When there are six or more people scheduled to attend a meeting, publish an agenda and exact times in advance. Stick to it. Have separate conversations take place outside the meeting. If two or three people can solve a problem, don't bother everyone else at the meeting. Randomly pick a person at the end to write up action steps assigned to each person.

3. Give everyone an assigned subject to present at most meetings. If anybody attends meetings merely to listen, ask them to leave and fill them in later. Meetings are for contributors, not audiences.

CHAPTER 25

Remove Physical Barriers

I was brought in to salvage Monument Industries in Broadfield, Nebraska, in 1984. The company made architectural marble ornaments and did well until the stone-cutter founder of the business died two years earlier.

He was replaced by his son. Two years after that, I was called in to rescue the company.

The founder's son was painfully shy and really didn't want to run the business. But he felt a sense of duty. So he took over and began to put his imprint on the company. He had a new office built in the back of the building. It had a private entrance. Within two years, profits disappeared and Monument Industries had to begin laying off some of its 300 employees.

When I arrived, I found that everyone had become as political and secretive as the founder's son. Production had expanded without talking to sales or accounting. Sales and accounting had appointed "liaisons" and "coordinators" to talk to each other.

That first day, two trucks unloaded finished slabs onto our dock. This wasn't right. We were supposed to send out finished slabs. Not take them. It turned out, of course, that they had been returned by troubled customers.

"What went wrong?" I asked the shipping foreman.

"Uh, ah, you'll have to get that from my supervisor," he said. The guy fidgeted from foot to foot as he looked away.

It had to come from his supervisor. This was like government. He knew. He was afraid to tell me. Not his responsibility.

INSIDE THE BUILDING was little more than a hallway of closed doors. My desk was buried under a pile of memos. All afternoon, I watched. The few times anyone talked, they were in furtive conversations, ducking their heads behind doors so as not to be seen. They all practically genuflected before me — not in honor, but in fear.

Before leaving that day, I went to the head of maintenance. "Take off every inside door tonight except for the restrooms and computer room. Stack them in the parking lot where everybody will see them for a couple of days, and then sell them."

"You must be kidding," said the head of maintenance.

"Not at all," I said.

Sure, it was theatrical. But this business was in dramatic trouble. Some show business was needed to open things up.

It helped. A month or so later a salesman from Standard Cutting, which made tools that carve granite, came into the building. For the previous two years, he had never gotten past the lobby. He had always come in, taken his orders in the lobby and then shuffled back to the parking lot. But on this visit, things were different. He went from office to office, getting to know our people, listening to their situations and explaining his.

Before he left, he sprang into my office, which didn't have a door. "It's as if I'd never been here before," he said. "This is a new company." He smiled. "You know, I did a week's worth of business in one day. There's no waiting now. There's no hesitating. I love that you got rid of the doors." He loved it so much he cut our prices by 10 percent. He suggested the cut. Him. I wasn't quick enough to ask.

"I can deal with you quick and straight now," he said.

THERE WAS MORE. One time, the vice-president of marketing pulled me aside. "Hey," he said, with a hopeful glint in his eye. I was hopeful too. The look on his face told me he was onto something good for the company. He was sincere. He said, "I hear you need a Cross pen refill. Here's one of mine," he said. So sincere, it was unbelievable.

Anytime you see a closed door, knock and stick your head in. If company business is being conducted, nobody should be embarrassed.

I couldn't hold back "Listen. You're the vice-president of marketing. It's your job to make sales grow," I said. He looked at me, surprised by my switch from the "safe" subject of my pen. So I went back to it. "I'm terrified that you think paying attention to my minor needs has any importance at all. I've failed tragically to communicate. Don't ever do anything like that again or we're both headed for failure. Your job is marketing, mine is to help you succeed."

He stood there with his mouth open for about 30 seconds. When what I said sunk in, he smiled faintly. "Fine," he said.

It was blunt, but he understood. In fact, after the shock he was happy with the change, happy to exist as an equal, happy to be set loose, finally, to the cause of sales.

ANOTHER MONUMENT INDUSTRIES example about what barriers can create was a guy named Terry Rowan. His job at Monument was to design and print pages of advertising that went into reference books. He was the company artist.

One of my first days, as I was surveying personnel, I asked someone, "Who is Terry's boss?" I was told he works for production.

I went to production. They told me he worked for sales.

I was curious, so I went to accounting. I found Terry's file. I wanted to look up how much Terry made and who had approved his pay. It turned out he hadn't enjoyed a raise in four years. His last raise was done by the previous sales manager.

I asked Terry. "Who is your boss?"

"I don't know," he said. "Nobody pays much attention as long as I get the catalogs out."

"Who fills you in on company objectives? Who helps you? Who gives you raises?"

"Nobody."

There were so many barriers that Terry became an island for years and nobody knew it. Nobody.

To keep the skipper in touch with the lighthouse:

1. Anytime you see a closed door, knock and stick your head in. Ask if everything is okay. If company business is being conducted, nobody should be embarrassed. Just keep doing this until everybody "gets it."

2. Eliminate assigned parking except for one spot — employee of the month, near the front door. The only way to get a good parking spot at a good company is to show up early. Close the executive lunchroom or open it to all.

3. Spend half of your time out of your office. Work in other people's areas. See what is going on and let everyone sense that you know and care. Don't screen calls; put direct lines into everyone's office. This saves time, cuts costs, simplifies phone bills, and keeps everybody in closer contact. Doors, guards, secretaries, and memos are little more than ways to avoid contact.

CHAPTER 26

Eliminate Sex

Office sex is blind. Love is blind. William Agee, chairman, proved that at Bendix when he lost all business perspective from an infatuation with his "protégé," Mary Cunningham.

Mary Cunningham was intelligent enough. So was William Agee. The trouble was that the two of them fell madly in lust, and, later, I suppose, in love, but in the meantime they lost track of what they were supposed to be doing for Bendix. They screwed . . . Bendix.

One year when I was at Graphic Arts Center, we contracted to print the Bendix annual report — thirty-two pages, 50,000 per hour. It was a good order so we loaded up a few railroad boxcars of paper and everything was in full motion when Bendix called. Cunningham had just seen the proofs of the report (proofs had been around our plant for three days) and she had a complaint.

I heard about it from our salesman. He took the call. When he hung up, he said, "We have to stop printing. Cunningham doesn't like Agee's picture. She likes him better when he doesn't wear his glasses."

We stopped the press.

A plane was hired to fly a photographer to Agee. The same backdrop was used again but Agee was now holding his glasses smartly, instead of wearing them. The whole rearranging, including stalled press time, cost $60,000. Neither Cunningham or Agee ever thought of the cost, even though both have business savvy and normally would know better. The money came from shareholders, who never knew of the minor miscellaneous expense.

Affairs are the ultimate betrayal of team spirit.

Affairs are the ultimate betrayal of team spirit, and yet inevitably happen with energetic people. If you can keep your crew servicing the ship, not each other, you won't sink. Here's how:

1. Make sexual harassment painful for the higher-ranking party. Race, politics, religion, and sex are not subjects at business. A superior never asks a subordinate of the opposite sex to dinner. (Opposite sex means same sex to homosexuals.) A superior certainly lunches with subordinates of the opposite sex, but never one more than others and does so more often in groups. Peers may ask co-workers for a date once. Never twice. Once turned down, don't even hint at it again.
2. When affairs develop within a department, transfer the higher ranking lovebird and don't make it a promotion. It is more the responsibility of the superior to control it.
3. Make sure your insurance doesn't get too liberal with its stress benefits or counseling. One company was disrupted by a couple in the sales force who were having an affair. They denied it, but both divorced their spouses and signed up for a year of stress counseling. Our premium jumped so high the next year that salary increases companywide had to drop by 1 percent. If the rest of the crew knew of that, there would have been a mutiny.

CHAPTER 27

Attack Drugs and Alcohol

Bill Madison did a little less work in later years and missed quite a few Mondays. But he was an experienced thinker and produced top-selling toys so most people ignored his breath and Rand McNally eyes, and they dismissed his never-relaxed demeanor as just a creative person's quirk. There were many clues but they were all ignored. And so was Madison's drinking problem.

He ran one section of toy design at Fischer-Price in East Aurora, New York. Two of his group's winners were the popcorn popper and the ring stack. Each still sells about a million pieces a year.

I was there from California. Fisher-Price had just acquired our small toy company and we were learning to fit our product development into their plans. Madison and I had dined once before and negotiated several times when he was a customer. The night before at dinner, we finished two bottles of Cabernet Sauvignon. Two of us, two bottles.

We had just finished three days of product review with the toy selection committee. The result of all that was that Fisher-Price had pruned the next year's new offering down to forty items from 110 proposals. This was about average. We had a couple of items to do; Madison's group had a dozen.

Decisions had been made and therefore all the accompanying tension had disappeared. So Bill said, "Hey, c'mon over for some drinks and we'll cook and hunker down and talk."

I went. In Orchard Park, just outside Buffalo, we followed a winding path through tall maple trees to a contemporary glass house with three fireplaces. Snow was falling when we pulled in the driveway, which was accented by spotlights. The house was cheery and so were we.

Bill's wife mixed a batch of rum toddies, and he started the grill on the enclosed patio. It was a beautiful winter night and Bill and his wife were in rare form.

We finished the toddies. I did my share, and a second pitcher appeared. Suddenly the fire was leaping about four feet out of the grill, licking at the rafters. Bill's wife noticed. Bill was standing near-by. His attention was elsewhere, but who knows where.

Mrs. Madison started screaming and Bill ran to the garage for a bag of sidewalk sand. He threw sand on the fire. It went out. His house was saved, though temporarily scarred. There was a big black smudge on the ceiling, about seven feet across. And the paint had bubbled up in a couple of places. "Oh well," laughed Madison.

Nothing had been done for Bill Madison until he tried to bite a customer.

We skipped dinner and instead had another round of toddies. Mrs. Madison brought out cheese and apples.

Bill didn't make it to work the next day. It was an

important day, as we had scheduled and budgeted for the forty items. His crew, as they had done many times before, covered for him. I was just embarrassed enough about the evening, and my part of it, to not mention it to anybody.

I participated, but with a few badly needed brain cells not receiving signals.

I THOUGHT ABOUT BILL later when I heard he had made a spectacle of himself at a toy buyers' dinner in New York City. There was an open bar at Delmonicos, a lot of schmoozing, and some of the key buyers from the biggest retail chains in the country. Bill Madison had known many of these people for thirty years.

At the dinner, as the drinks flowed and flowed, Bill became much louder than everybody else and a salesman quietly asked Bill to go to his room. The dining room was about three quarters full but there was still time for Bill to walk away relatively unnoticed. Instead, he had another drink, then another, and then climbed up on a table on all fours and started barking like a dog. Then, between fits of laughter, he tried to bite one of the customers.

Nothing had been done for Bill Madison until he tried to bite a customer. By then it was too late. He was fired, although the company gave him a generous severance payment, and they paid for a rehabilitation program for him. He's probably either dry or dead today. I've never heard. There's such embarrassment and loss of dignity in these deals that nobody stays in touch.

It's not about being a watchdog every moment of your workers' lives. What they do off the job is their business. This is about productivity and safety.

To keep your crew off the grog:

1. Put in an anonymous employee-assistance program. This is a switch from the last chapter, where you are advised against offering counseling for stress. Counseling for stress

costs you money. Counseling for drugs and alcohol dependence saves you money.

2. Face reality. Your business has drug and alcohol problems. All do. The worst policy is a vague policy, next worse is an unpublished one. It's management's job to spell out exactly what the company will do to help with substance abuse and what is expected of the employee in overcoming it.

3. Alcohol problems are easier to spot for those of us born in 1942 or before. It's our drug of choice, our pal. When it interferes with work, talk to the employee about it immediately. If you're middle-aged, you probably don't understand drugs and the telltale signs. Do yourself a favor and learn. Accidents, erratic behavior, puffy and runny eyes, sniffles, and jitters could mean nothing. You can't wonder, especially around equipment. Check the restrooms and keep your eyes open in the parking lot. People and companies die from this stuff.

CHAPTER 28

Quit Gambling

There was a cash manager who used his company's money like chips at a casino. I'll call this cash manager Ben Feders and I won't bother to make up a name for the company. The company is on the New York Stock Exchange, and it was Ben's job to manage a lot of cash.

Each day, Ben had to guess how much cash to put into short-term deposits, how much into long term, and when to borrow just a little. He was not at all a gregarious Vegas type, yet he played the market like a high-stakes game. He put his company's money where his mouth was. He borrowed heavily when he thought rates might rise soon and he stuffed cash into fixed rates when he thought they might drop.

It was a regular talent show. Even though Ben was a shy, nervous guy with glasses and spare batteries for his calculator, there was something about him that took on the air of a gambler. He was The Kid, and people in the hallways of the company looked up to him in the same odd way people look to professional athletes who have instincts most can't fathom.

TOM WOLFE called it "the right stuff," and it was apparently in Feders's blood. That's what everyone thought. It was fascinating as this nervous guy became almost charismatic within the corporate culture.

He set up a display that he changed every day. He charted his projections, and he graphed the company's plans. Soon, purchasing, production, and sales began consulting monthly with Ben. Then weekly, and finally daily.

There were daily meetings with Ben in front holding court and changing forecasts. It was entertaining, and sometimes his focus would go out to more abstract things, like Ben's read on America's economic problems.

"Everybody's worried about the national debt," he observed one time, "but it doesn't matter. That's just money we owe ourselves. Our problem is the shift from being a creditor nation to a debtor nation. That displays a fundamental weakness that no amount of intervention from the Fed can ever fix." Huh?

Ben went from cash manager to company economist to global soothsayer in just two years.

It was marvelous. He should have sold tickets. Sometimes it seemed as if he did. When dealers came through, part of every tour was to visit Ben's war room — a jungle of computer screens, printouts, and jangling phones that could autodial bankers across the country. It was in this room that decisions were made to loan and borrow, short term and long term.

Gambling goes on in every business that operates without guidelines.

The community college invited Ben to speak about cash management to finance majors. He spoke every semester. One year, he was president of the Financial Executives

Club — a group of CFOs and analysts who gathered monthly to discuss interest rates, banking, and bonds. No whoopee cushions there. In that atmosphere, Ben was the star attraction.

He was an expert — the wizard from his particular company, and no one ever questioned his intelligence or instinct for cash management. All you had to do was listen to him talk, spin his magic.

BUT ONE DAY the CEO of this company retired, and an outside guy was hired. First, the new CEO revitalized research, lowered inventories, and made a change in marketing. Then he took a look at cash management and the wizard of the markets.

The CEO asked the CPA firm to calculate the difference between the wizard's system and a more conservative plan of simply putting excess cash in CDs at prevailing rates and borrowing only at the amounts needed for the time needed.

The difference? Try $14 million. There would have been an extra $14 million in the till if four years hadn't been wasted trying to outguess the market.

It cost even more. Since the company was paid a week later than all the competitors — because of the time spent in Ben's office, speculating instead of collecting — there was a week's lost cash, and the interest expense on it, every week. This was an even greater loss than the speculation tragedies.

Ben Feders's gambling goes on in every business that operates without guidelines. There are controllers guessing the prime rate, plant managers guessing on fuel futures, production people betting on leases, and credit folks speculating on the economy. They're all distracted and therefore less efficient.

It's more fun than work, but it's not the right stuff. There are ways to swagger by loosening or tightening credit, borrowing long term or short term, depositing the same, signing long-term leases instead of buying, or vice versa, setting inventory levels, or negotiating energy contracts.

Business has enough risk without creating more. There's not one business in the world that has succeeded based on those bets, but plenty have been sucked under water by gambling on the side. Here's how to stay dry:

1. Each year, get everybody together and agree on a plan for interest rates, inflation, and your commodity prices. Then everybody takes a blood oath to make every decision based on that consensus. If things change dramatically, call a second meeting to adjust the guidelines. Will those guides be exactly right? Never. But neither will others, and this gets the group acting consistently and eliminates distractions.

2. In areas where you must speculate, as with pension funds, put equal amounts into stocks, bonds, real estate, and CDs. Never buy or sell more than 10 percent of the portfolio in a year, and do that only to maintain the balance. Use outside managers to do this for you and pick them based on lowest management fee. They're no better at this than anyone else, so concentrate on simple administration, straight guidelines, and spartan costs.

3. With credit, determine what level of losses you must experience to be competitive in the marketplace. If you can boast of a perfect credit record, you've missed some good business somewhere. Make sure write-offs and rolled-over debts get counted as bad; when you are pushing collections those are a couple of easy ways to lose chunks of money while appearing to bring receivables back in line.

Send God Back to Church

The famous singing family called. That was the message on my desk at Montron, the toy company. That's right, Ma and Pa Smileyvoice wanted to talk business with us.

They wanted to talk with us about our toy movie viewers, in which a viewer could watch a three-minute cartridge just by turning a crank. Originally, we planned to limit the marketing only to cartoon cartridges. But we made mistakes in startup and therefore were still paying for some tooling that had to be scrapped. Although sales were good, margins were not strong enough to cover past sins. So we chased other sales.

One popular series was a CPR set of cartridges that the Red Cross bought and sold with every training dummy and instruction kit. In addition, a couple of pharmaceutical companies bought the viewers to show doctors and patients how to apply a new glaucoma treatment and how to apply severe burn bandages.

WE WERE LOOKING for business when the Smileyvoices called looking to make a cartridge and buy 5,000 viewers and cartridges. They wanted to make a cartridge of the milk-and-cookie group's recent European tour, and they wanted it to feature their youngest son and cherubic-faced daughter.

The package called for us to edit the film down to a three-minute cartridge. Over the phone, I quoted $2,500 to edit, $2,000 for the printing plates, and $7 per viewer and cartridge, plus boxing.

God was on our side, she said. It was a good thing too because, later, Mrs. Smileyvoice told me she couldn't pay our bill.

"That's a little steep, but this is just a start," said Mrs. Smileyvoice, ever the negotiating businesswoman. "We have 200,000 very active fans. Can you do better with larger quantities after this test?"

"Sell these and you've paid for the editing and plates forever. Double the quantity and the price drops a dollar," I quoted. They bought it.

I flew from our San Francisco office to their suite at Tropicana Hotel in Las Vegas. When I arrived, they were mostly lounging around, but Mrs. Smileyvoice was all business. She wanted to ensure that the youthful son and the wholesome daughter, who were more popular than the older kids, were featured in the cartridge. "Put their brothers in the background," she instructed.

She had a contract ready. I read it and it was just as we had agreed over the phone. I signed it and started to leave, since our business was complete.

Before I could leave, but as my signature dried, Mrs. Smileyvoice asked me to pray. Actually, she said, "One moment, young man," in her best motherly tone. "Let us pray for success before you leave." She had a grave look.

It had been some time since I prayed, and somehow bowing my head while she delivered the words in her mirrored leather Las Vegas room wasn't how I remembered it. I had nothing against God, it's just that her God and mine weren't exactly tennis partners. But I bowed anyway and murmured and nodded in the interest of commerce.

God was on our side, she said. It was a good thing too because, later, Mrs. Smileyvoice told me she couldn't pay our bill. She assured me, "The Lord is testing us right now," and then added, "I just don't know where the money is going to come from."

Well, in the end His Fanclubness came through and people were moved to buy Youthful Boy and Wholesome Girl Smileyvoice toy film projectors. They sold the first 5,000 projectors, and they reordered.

When your vendor proclaims religious fervor, double-check his invoices.

Despite their assurances that our prayers had come true, I insisted on the money up front for the reorder. I even had the gall to ask for payment on the amount due from the previous batch. A miracle happened and the money came.

We cashed the check and delivered the second order two months later, proving the Lord sometimes works in mysterious ways.

Religion is private. When your vendor proclaims religious fervor, double-check his or her invoices.

Here's how to keep religion in the church and off your decks:

1. Make it clear that your company respects the individual above all. Any intrusion on individual beliefs will not be tolerated. No prayers. No invitations to religious services. Of course, weddings, funerals, and bar mitzvahs are fine. But nothing more. Run a business, not a house of worship.

2. The pursuit of profit is often attacked by those seeking to impose their beliefs. Put up a defense against this by pointing out, in policy statements, that profits prove two things. Profits prove that the organization is paying taxes to help support the community and nation, not just sucking up free services. Next point out that profits come from providing services that are valued higher than the cost of the labor and goods consumed to create them. To not profit, therefore, means the organization consumes more than it produces, which makes it parasitic.

3. Remember that religion comes in different guises with names like Amway, United Way, PTA, Girl Scout cookies, and political action committees. None of these have any right to intrude. Employees come to the job to work, and employers pay for these efforts. Anything else is an invasion.

PART 4

THE HORIZON: Working with the World

CHAPTER 30

Slash Consulting

A basketball coach invented the hand-held movie viewer. He thought it would be a good training tool to help players visualize different moves and shots.

He brought it to us at Honeywell, and we were intrigued so we put our ad agency on it. They recommended a consulting firm, and soon we hired them to do $4,000 worth of research, half paid up front and half upon completion of the surveys and report.

Part of the deal, and the more expensive part, was creating a set of handmade prototypes that worked well enough to hold and use. The consultants came through with the prototypes and then they set out to consult.

TWO TABLES were set up at opposite ends of the walkways into the Apache Plaza in Minneapolis. Interviewers sat with samples while one stood soliciting interviews. Each three-minute interview included questions about the product, choice of films, and what they would expect to pay. The usual rough information about income and occupation was inferred from zip codes.

A trailer was parked in the lot for more in-depth interviews with a dozen willing subjects who were "willing" partly because they were given theater tickets. But the consultants were practically scientists, they claimed, and they aimed to prove they could unlock the key to success for this particular product, the hand-held movie viewer. They used their scientific modus operandi of asking broad, probing questions about attitude, plus collecting information about other products owned and not owned. Occupations and hobbies were noted. They also interviewed on weekends and evenings to ensure a broad cross-section of people.

This was the consultants' conclusion: "This is a serious educational product. The biggest possible mistake you can make is to treat it as a toy." They also talked about the need for some point-of-purchase demonstrator, since it was an unfamiliar product.

Development of a full library of skill films was the key. The software had to sell the hardware. The message from the broad cross section of people was clear: This is a hot new product, but only if it is treated as a serious educational device.

Even though a lot of people at Honeywell were excited, it would have taken two tons of development money and the timing wasn't right, so we passed.

THE INVENTOR went back to Northern California, where a leading venture capitalist who also happened to own a sporting goods store liked the idea. The venture capitalist told several people from Honeywell he would risk another $1 million in startup expense if they would personally join the effort. They joined. John Belden, the Honeywell sales manager, quit and moved to California to run the startup. Two of my best friends in the marketing department left to join him.

The first $1 million slipped away pretty fast. Johnny Unitas was hired to do the football films. Jean Shrimpton did a series on makeup and modeling. Arnold Palmer handled the golf series. There were a dozen different subjects covered and filmed, each one with several film cartidges. The dozen celebrity subjects cost quite a bit, and so did the marketing.

Tests were set up on the West Coast in sporting goods stores and department stores. All the bases were covered. Newspaper, television, and radio ads were timed to coincide, and displays in the stores were each well stocked to service the broad cross section of buyers they expected.

Consulting is the great wimp-out of business.

But the buyers never showed. The problem was that the only people who were interested were the broad cross section who were willing to answer probing personal questions for theater tickets. That's a minuscule cross section.

So the company altered its strategy and tried more advertising, different advertising, lower prices, coupons, sample giveaways to local schools, and direct mail offers. Nothing worked well, and another million in cash evaporated. Layoffs started. Merchandise was returned and stacked in the warehouse.

About January 1972, the company's UPS bill for return shipments exceeded that for outgoing shipments. That was special.

AND THEN, BY CHANCE, Belden met people from Disney, who gave Belden some Mickey Mouse cartoons to try. Disney had no competing products in the category, liked his product, and gave Belden the rights to their cartoon library in exchange for a 7 percent royalty.

By the time Belden hooked up with Disney, he had a handful of workers left and there was just enough money to meet three more payrolls and buy some Mickey Mouse labels and packaging.

And just like that, the company rebounded. There was no advertising and no special giveaways, but there was something better — a product people wanted.

The investor put more money in, and better cartoons and packaging were developed. Within two years, an $8 million business was born.

But it was delayed two years and cost an extra $3 million. In addition, several careers were disrupted and John Belden's hair prematurely grayed. There was one cause for all these problems: a consulting report that confirmed exactly the wrong strategy.

The main difference between you and consultants is that you know more about your business, cost less to analyze it, and are responsible for the results. The captain goes down with the ship; the consultant rows back to dry land to seek more business from others.

Consulting is the great wimp-out of business. It puts decisions elsewhere, delays them, and costs more. Managers know how to find what is wrong, or they shouldn't be managers.

Here's how to ensure consultants will feel a part of your ship:

1. Put half of the consultants' pay on a performance basis. If the goals aren't met, no pay. Use consultants only when you have to know about new areas or unfamiliar technology or markets. Otherwise, you're chickening out.

2. If, as often is the case, you're hiring a consultant to tell you what you want to hear so you can defend a move to owners or employees or customers, don't pay on performance and don't pay until you have the final report. Let's not kid ourselves about what you are doing. Every consulting firm spends most of their time on projects like this.

Just sell them personally on your viewpoint so they can spit it back up with some enthusiasm.

3. If you are looking for an honest appraisal, including an evaluation of your own management effectiveness, pay the consultants in advance. You can't expect honesty if their last check isn't due until after they submit the report.

CHAPTER 31

Manage the Lawyers

Knight Protective Industries was the defendant for one primary reason. Knight Protective was guilty. The complaint was trademark infringement and from what I could tell after becoming CEO in 1990, Knight had infringed upon a Reno burglar alarm company that also had Knight as its name. Knight Protective of North Hollywood, California, is a national burglar alarm company with accounts from New York City to Honolulu.

The previous year, Knight fought the case legally on its merits and lost. The legal bill in 1989 was $300,000, which made us think the cost of the battle was more than any possible cost of a loss. As a result of the case, there was an injunction against us prohibiting the use of the trademark in Nevada.

Knight appealed, challenging the premise of the case because it was filed two years after the infringement. Prior to going to the appeals court, the other company filed another suit against us claiming violation of the injunction and therefore contempt of court. We went into a preliminary hearing in Reno's State Superior Court.

The judge heard both sides give brief arguments, and then he shook his head. He stood up. "It seems rather silly to take this any further, don't you think?" he offered. "Here's what I'm going to do. I'm going to leave the room for about an hour. Let's see if you two can act like adults and reach some kind of settlement." And the judge left the room.

THE PLAINTIFF focused his smoldering eyes on me. "I'll see you bankrupt if it takes every penny I have," he hissed.

I was startled. "I'll tell you what," I said, "we don't have any more money than what I already offered to settle. So how about this: We'll give you 20 percent of our company on top of the cash offer of $100,000 we already made." I smiled. "You can have a seat on the board."

"What's the stock worth?" he asked, sarcastically.

"About a negative $2 per share. Once we suck you into owning some newly issued shares, that drops to only a negative $1.60 per share. Gives you a chance to share our debts. If you win in court, we can't pay so you lose. If you lose, you lose. I can make that offer to you on the spot, without even checking with my board, because if you accept, we've shifted some debt to you and the value of our holdings goes up."

He walked out.

I didn't care, even though he had won the first round. There were three weaknesses to his case. One, he had neglected to complain or even bring up the infringement for two years.

Profits are inversely proportional to legal bills unless you're in some fake business that's regulated.

Two, and he didn't know this yet, we had documented sales trends from his hardware suppliers that showed his sales increased when we started advertising in his territory. This concurred with his complaint, which stated customers called his sales office citing our advertising and thinking his company was ours. (This says a lot about our advertising, but that's another chapter.) That fact made his chances stronger but reduced his potential for collecting damages. It helped his case because a key to winning trademark infringement is proving confusion in the marketplace. But he was apparently benefiting from the confusion.

The third weakness, as I had told him before, was quite serious. Knight Protective was in the middle of a traumatic turnaround and had no cash to pay any significant damages.

THE PLAINTIFF RETURNED and five minutes later so did the judge. The plaintiff didn't say much but you could tell he was ballistic, on a hair trigger when the judge asked what happened. His pudgy, balding lawyer simply told the judge that there was no hope for an out-of-court settlement. The lawyer jangled change in his pocket when he talked.

Knight beat this charge after a one-week trial. Then the Appellate Court unanimously overturned the first decision, which we had appealed. The appellate judges agreed that the original complaint was filed far too late. At this stage, with a unanimous appellate decision, it was 100–1 that another appeal would work or even be heard by the Supreme Court. But we were not dealing with a rational being here, so we offered $30,000 to settle forever. He accepted. Our legal bill was only $10,000 this time, compared with $300,000 the year before.

OUR CARDINAL SIN was that we let our lawyers get mad, and we cheered them on initially. Instead of letting logic intervene, the other side counterattacked. We were spurred on when our lawyers got mad because then we got mad, which made them madder. And all the time the opponent was doing the same. It wasn't legal; it was a personal affront.

At one point their attorney threatened to punch our attorney, who welcomed it with a macho, "Go ahead, take your best shot!"

They both took their best shots, all right. With our money. And we let them.

Profits are inversely proportional to legal bills unless you're in some fake business that's regulated. America's Cup recently proved that boating with lawyers isn't boating, it's boring. Boating without litigation is fun. So it goes in business. Here's how to settle, not fight:

1. Never buy legal work without an estimate in advance. This will cut your legal bills by about one third for conventional work. Shop around. For unconventional jobs, and there aren't many of these, review the billing weekly and review exactly what is being done and why. There's not a law firm in the world that posts its partners' wins and losses, yet every firm knows precisely how much every partner managed to bill clients last year.

2. Always test your firm's beliefs by offering some form of contingency before going after somebody. Also try incentives for a winning defense. It doesn't have to be a 100 percent contingency. You can split out-of-pocket expenses without markup and let the firm keep 25 percent of the winnings. If the fire disappears from their eyes, you know the case isn't worth pursuing. (Don't shop this offer around; you can always find some firm that is desperate for work and will take your deal just to cover expenses.)

3. When you have a legal bill that seems outrageous, don't pay it. Pay what's right. Attorneys can't sue clients without seriously boosting their malpractice rates. Since attorneys invented the concept of malpractice, there's a nice touch of justice to that.

CHAPTER 32

Woo the Bankers

At U.S. Press, we started getting the bankers ready to push money at us two years before we needed it.

At the time, we just saw it as a chance to cultivate relationships with several cash pools. Intermark, our parent company, held a "Banker's Day" at least once a year and U.S. Press always made a presentation at the meetings. We showed sales growth, cash flow, and profit, and then we would tour a plant and let representatives of three different banks see, touch, and smell the equipment. Bankers love to remind themselves that they are dealing with something more than numbers.

So we did it up. When our new Toshiba press was installed and purring in Portland, we let the bankers climb three stories of catwalks for a bird's-eye view. At the top, we set up a table of coffee and doughnuts, and we watched Bloomingdale's Christmas catalog whiz through the 270-foot-long press. There were cranes loading two-ton rolls of paper in one end and forklifts removing catalogs at the other. We had a unique time with the bankers. They never sipped coffee and munched doughnuts in such a vibrant setting before. Then we demonstrated more wizardry. We programmed the computer to print out catalogs addressed to them at their banks, and then we presented it to them before they left as new friends. That's right. No requests, just friends. *Oh, and check out all the neat stuff that we do.*

Another year, we brought the group into a prepress area where they watched a technician change the color of a Mercedes proof by hitting keys on a keyboard. Proofs were pulled both ways so one banker received a brochure with a teal Mercedes, and the next banker received a maroon one. It was fun for all. And, as always, key figures were presented and handed out so the bankers had a basic grasp of the business.

Continental Bank, Bank of America, Union and First Interstate Bank were all participants. At each meeting, U.S. Press sat with a different banker to keep up an idea of competition for any future business.

When we were in downtown Los Angeles, we stopped for a visit and a quick update. Usually we would be calling on ARCO or Western Airlines, or Georgio, or Honda. We could show the banks what we were printing for clients of ours who were sometimes also theirs. Soon these meetings became a forecast for when we intended to go public. As a subsidiary of Intermark, we always borrowed from Intermark. But when we would go public, we could need our own bank cash, we explained in optimistic tones.

THEY LISTENED. They started wondering "when," not "if" they could loan us some money, they knew us so well. But we didn't want to borrow too soon.

We waited, and in 1982 the market dipped and caught U.S. Press in a margin squeeze. We dropped our prices 4 and 5 percent just to keep the new presses busy. Then we slashed costs to the marrow just to make a paper-thin profit. At the end of the year, our meager earnings made the company look less attractive.

But within six months things came back. We went out on our own and three banks were clamoring to loan us money.

During the downturn, we scrambled for business and made some painful cuts to operating expenses. We spun off marginal subsidiaries. And, always more shameful, we cut people. That's how we survived.

Instead of cursing the bankers when times are tough, try romancing them when things are good.

We rebounded sharply, though, because of our actions during the troubles. We continued meeting with the bankers and telling them about the current and forecasted state of our business. We told them more about our business when we were troubled than we did during good times.

When the economy turned, Linda Ariaza of Union Bank said this: "Usually silence is our first sign of trouble. You guys are just the opposite. It's refreshing."

So was her attitude. When we finally asked for money, Linda smiled and came back two weeks later with $10 million at prime plus 1 percent. Two weeks for a new customer. New, but not unknown.

Bankers cannot make more than a few percentage points on the money loaned, but they can lose it all. That's why they're jumpy. Help them relax by making them familiar with your business.

Woo the bankers: It is their money you're using. Try something different. Instead of cursing them when times are tough, try romancing them when things are good.

To keep the bankers sponsoring your fleet:

1. Get to know your banker's boss. There's enough

turnover at the account level that you'll find yourself starting all over every two years if you don't. Introduce several of your key officers regularly so the bankers can get information from several sources. Always be acquainted with several different banks, to protect yourself when your banker changes jobs and forgets you. Talk to bankers that fund your competitors. They think they already understand your business.

2. Every quarter, give the bankers background information on your industry. Give it to them whether or not you need money. Give them quarterly financial statements and talk with them about the future. Soon, your bankers will anticipate your needs and ask you if you need a loan. It's much better than if they knew nothing about you and are surprised with your request for quick cash.

3. When things go bad, give the bankers more information than normal. This forces you to really tighten up your actions. The bankers will feel a stronger bond when you pull it through. (And if you don't pull through, it doesn't matter anyway.) When bankers see you beat a tough time, they see you as more of a worthwhile investment — and less of a risk.

CHAPTER 33

Use the CPA as More Than an Accountant

"You know, it would sort of put icing on the cake if somebody would buy this business now," mused Bob Jacobsen. It was a thankful time for Jacobsen and for the company he owned, Checks To-Go.

Jacobsen was already very comfortable, having created a tax software company that Burroughs Computer acquired in the 1970s. Jacobsen and his offspring created Checks To-Go as a hobby in 1976, and I was hired as CEO in 1986.

Checks To-Go went through two CEOs, and it required cash to keep afloat every year until the turnaround we did in 1986, when we redirected the business. (Chapter 16 told of one way it was redirected, and Chapters 17 and 24 gave more details.)

Finally, in 1987, Checks To-Go was gushing profits and Jacobsen remarked how wonderful it would be to find a buyer. It was nothing urgent. We didn't need money. In fact, Checks To-Go was now a money machine in the fast-growing PC-peripherals market. But the Jacobsens were typically relieved and somewhat disbelieving owners of a recovered business. They didn't want to test their luck.

SO WE STARTED looking, quietly. Finding a buyer would be tricky. Several competitors would probably be interested, but if they knew we were for sale, a few would spread the word among our clients that we were troubled and for sale.

We went to an investment banker called Geneva. Geneva specialized in small businesses, and they were doing well enough to be ostentatious. They drove up to our comfortable adobe building in El Cajon, California, in a Mercedes and a BMW, and when they got out of the cars all were wearing designer suspenders, a sure sign that they were overpriced. After we talked briefly, they pulled at those suspenders and told us they needed $20,000 to do the preliminary analysis of our business: an appraisal and optimistic projections.

We passed. We called Price Waterhouse, our acccounting firm, and put together a plan. We drafted a letter that they would send from their Los Angeles headquarters instead of the local office. It was to go to every competitor and possible strategic partner imaginable. The letter described the size, profits, growth rate, and asking price for Checks To-Go, but it did not name the company. It gave a general description of the service, but there were no specifics. The letter hinted at probable economies of scale that this acquirer might expect.

Nothing happened.

Auditors are your best outside advisors.

We went back to Price Waterhouse and suggested they do a second letter to the same list. Since CPA firms, especially in the Big Six, have credibility at stake in everything they do, we merely restated the sales pitch in the second letter and sent it to the same list. Price Waterhouse didn't ask, but we insisted on paying their costs plus a markup.

The second letters went out and nothing happened. We paid the Los Angeles office about $1,000 to cover the partner's time to look over and approve the mailing as well as the cost of the postage, clerical time, and stationery.

We tried a third letter, repeating the proposition. Understandably, Price Waterhouse's enthusiasm was on the wane. This wasn't their business. But they were serving us as a client and luckily we were paying their expenses, making it easier for them to humor us. We got a live response from RapidForms on the East Coast. "We'd like to learn a little more," their CEO said to Price Waterhouse. He signed a confidentiality agreement and our accounting firm told him more.

Their executive vice-president flew out to visit and a slow-paced mating ritual began.

Another company, Wescert of Denver, became interested in Checks To-Go at the same time. Strangely, their interest came from wanting to get into PC supplies and had nothing to do with our efforts. They had heard reports about the resurgence of Checks To-Go. When Wescert heard about Rapidforms' interest, and vice versa, both sides became even more interested — lemming lust.

We expressed appropriate surprise, delight, and humility at being pursued but in our best hard-to-get tone explained that life was quite good as is. Wescert couldn't stand it and made a cash offer of eight times book value. We pretended our acceptance was reluctant.

Price Waterhouse probably doubled our sale price by finding another credible suiter without making us hang out a "For Sale" sign by advertising or publicly listing the business. Price Waterhouse's credibility helped. And they got more work to help in the final transaction. They made several years' fees in closing the deal. That's fair.

Auditors are your best outside advisers. They know your numbers and, more important, how your numbers stock up against the rest of the world's. Better than you, they know how you're doing.

Your CPA firm is like your navigator. You may not always like what they report but their service is often your best way to win the race, and they often see trouble before the captain has a clue. Here's how to use them better:

1. When a controller or CFO leaves, keep the position empty and bring your CPA firm in an extra three days to help close the books each month. It will cost you about half of the old salary and it adds objectivity.

2. Before each annual audit, have your CPA firm's partner agree to spend extra time looking for a couple of extra things, such as possible cost reductions; or have the firm compare your management and operations to similar clients — reporting your relative strengths.

3. When selling a division or the company, use your CPA rather than a glossy investment banker. Your CPA understands your business better than an investment banker ever will, charges less, and has earned more credibility. CPAs are less prone to designer suspenders.

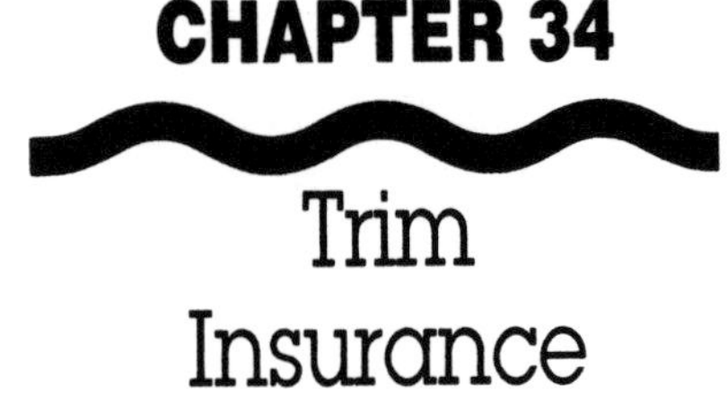

CHAPTER 34

Trim Insurance

Sunrise Capital spent $11 million to buy Pacific Metals, and Warren Smith got a Ford, two fistfuls of cash, and a life insurance policy. Smith was happy.

He grew up in the business that his Dad started and ran for forty years. He knew *everything*. He knew the cycles of metal prices. He knew how to negotiate commercial power rates and he knew where to find the best trucking prices by season. He swam in the veins of this business.

When Sunrise Capital's board, where I was director, agreed to buy Pacific Metals, part of the deal was to lease him a new car and to take out a half-million-dollar life insurance policy. Smith insisted on a maroon Ford Taurus with a tape deck and the bigger engine. We agreed.

When we talked about the life insurance, Smith introduced us to his agent, who handled all his business and had for years. We smiled and later introduced Smith to our broker, Johnson & Higgins. With trepidation, Smith let us stay with Johnson & Higgins.

THE ACQUISITION went through, and Smith got his maroon Taurus. We took over his company under his supervision. A month later, Smith came in to talk to us about his insurance.

"I'm taking a loss on some real estate this year, so I would rather have the income than the insurance," he said. "Is it too late to change back?"

Our CFO, Bob Milliken, called Johnson & Higgins, who were able to undo the contract without penalty and get the cash back. We sent the check for $80,000 to Smith.

A few days later, the phone rang and it was Smith, loudly protesting about his payment. "Where's the rest of the money?," he bellowed into the phone.

"That's all the policy cost," said Milliken.

"Nope. Nope. Nope," machine gunned Smith. "I spent half a day with my New York Life agent. I saw the numbers. Hell, I still know 'em. That policy cost you $100,000 minimum."

Milliken took a deep breath. He started to explain. "We bought exactly what we agreed to contractually. You signed it. That's the coverage you had, with the same quality rating. The only difference is that we found it for $80,000. What's more, Johnson & Higgins spotted ways to knock another $30,000 off Pacific Metal's annual insurance expense without reducing your coverage anywhere."

"I don't believe it."

A delicate series of explanations and proof followed. Johnson & Higgins managed our insurance. They bid every policy, were constantly in the market shopping for other clients, and always knew where the values were. Smith's premium expense had crept out of line over the years. It was the only leak in an otherwise tight ship. His view of insurance as a commodity, as opposed to a service that has all kinds of price variances, was costing him big time. It was the only place in his business where he was not getting top value.

SMITH NEVER ever totally believed it. Part of his disbelief may have been frustration at the realization he had overpaid by so much for so many years. He never said as much. He refused to discuss it. For years afterward, he just kept mumbling that we conned him out of $20,000.

Of course, he ended up resigning prematurely from Pacific Metals. It was too bad, because he knew the business better than anyone. His ongoing input would have helped. But his outlook was jaundiced, so we parted.

Insurance is a lifeboat if and when you need it. The payments, though, are barnacles. Here's how to gain adequate protection without dragging in the water:

1. Use a broker who shops for insurance without getting paid commissions. There are values and ripoffs, just like any other product or service. The value of any coverage goes down as the commission rate and a regular agent's enthusiasm goes up.

2. Buy less. Buy as little as you can. Companies with good coverage get sued more often for more money than those without heavy coverage. It's lawyer bait. Raise every deductible. Self-insure. Don't cover your company against the improbable accident, no matter how cheap. Always remember, insurance companies take in more from premiums than they pay back in damage payments. That's how they get their names on all those skyscrapers.

3. If, in a weak moment, you are struck by fear of losing some of your life's work due to an accident or lawsuit and therefore are considering raising your insurance, take a breath and consider setting up a more generous retirement plan outside your business instead. This survives catastrophies in ways that no amount of insurance protection or lawyers can provide.

CHAPTER 35

Challenge the Do-Gooders

In 1991, after a dramatic restructuring, a modest level of profitability was reached at Knight Protective and so the company added two community-oriented policies. Knight first added partial payment of wages for those employees called to jury duty. The second policy was to give the option of one paid day off a year to do charitable work of the employee's choice.

The rub was, nobody took the day off. We were trying to give something to the community in wages and workers and time, but nobody took an interest.

In the wake of the 1992 Los Angeles Rodney King riots, relief efforts were solicited daily. Still, no one volunteered so finally I called the Red Cross and volunteered for a day in the riot zone.

I WENT TO their headquarters building in downtown Los Angeles The people there were all social and sincere. They provided me with a map, a large coffee urn, ten pounds of coffee, two cartons of Doritos, a case of Evian bottled water, two dozen boxes of Nabisco crackers, and a late-model station wagon to haul it in. I was given large Red Cross stickers — one each for the front and back of my shirt, I suppose, in part, so I wouldn't be shot, in part to score points for the Red Cross.

They gave me directions to a relief outpost in a Methodist church in South-Central Los Angeles. It was a Hispanic–Korean neighborhood.

My job was to take the food and coffee in, set it up, and then hang around for a few hours. "Stick around and be seen," they told me.

The church was easy to find. A line of 300 or so people — 99 percent Korean — pointed right at it. There was no shade at 10 A.M. and the sun was brutal. The wait to get inside was about two hours.

Once inside, they filled out forms in a process that somehow managed to take another two hours. I found the manager for the Federal Emergency Management Agency (FEMA). He hadn't missed many meals and was a chain-smoking swell of neuroses.

"Get all that stuff in the back here," he said, almost surreptitiously. "We need to keep it away from the crowd. We don't want them just taking it."

I helped bring everything in because heaven forbid that people in need get things from a charity group that is there to give. I was there only a few hours. I figured they were full-timers.

I HUNG AROUND as instructed. I talked with a relaxed psychological worker. She was sipping coffee and eating a Danish, sitting with three other volunteers who were also small-talking. The psychological worker explained to me that many of the people in the neighborhood — some of the 300 in line — had suffered stress and needed referrals for help.

She told me how stressful everything was for everyone. She took a bite of her Danish. Then she told me that the four of them at that table had each worked 21 straight days. I was there for four hours, and they drank a lot of coffee in that time. Never in that time did one of them talk to a single person waiting.

Two workers from the Fair Housing and Unemployment Agency set up an information table at one corner of the room. The woman worked on needlepoint and the man completed the gender stereotype by settling in with a dozen sports magazines. There was nothing else to do.

In the other corner, there were four workers from the Small Business Administration staffing a loan-application table. There was no one there, and the four sat telling dirty jokes.

She told me how stressful everything was for everyone. She took a bite of her Danish.

At another table, there were twenty lines processing relief loan application forms. There were twenty volunteers, but only one line was moving. Apparently, only one of the volunteers understood the application forms enough to be efficient at processing them. In the time this one volunteer processed ten completed forms, the other nineteen volunteers did a total of three.

The setup was astonishing. It seemed then that my coworkers would be giving more to society by working directly than by volunteering. Just as I was thinking this, an inspection team from Washington arrived.

Six well-groomed young bureaucrats marched to the FEMA manager's desk. Their intent leader got right to the point: "How many applicants do you have? How many are being processed? What can we do to help?"

The manager thanked the young bureacrat and explained that he was stretched out, "but I have a fine group of volunteers and we can handle it."

"Well, we're proud of you," said the high-intensity

Fed. "Please express our gratitude to all your wonderful helpers," he added at five decibels.

They shook hands and that was it.

THIS WAS ONLY a one-day experience. But it was eye opening and educational and if every employee did just one day a year, these charitable organizations just might start to get productive under the scrutiny, and for-profit employees would feel good about helping.

A little company-sponsored charity builds a more profitable attitude within the company, by helping employees learn to live outside themselves and support others. Teamwork feeds on that.

Every profitable company should do some charitable work. You learn a lot by getting out into it every once in a while and seeing more than the cameras and words of the media capture. Much "good work" is waste. Having life preservers on deck means nothing unless, once in a while, you see that they float.

Test your life preservers these three ways:

1. Don't make cash contributions to any charity. Instead, give time and effort. If they can't use your help but want your cash, you have to wonder.

2. When your company is profitable, pay employees enough for jury duty so they can do it with minimal sacrifice. Many business executives serve on the YMCA board, United Way, and school fund raisers, yet duck the real work of jury duty. That's why too many court decisions are made by the retired and the bored.

3. Create profits first. If you don't, you're not paying taxes and therefore are a parasite. Everybody uses public streets. Chances are some of your employees use public schools. This is not to suggest that those schools and streets are well managed (that's another book), but if you're using them, you ought to help pay. The only way to do that is to make money to pay taxes.

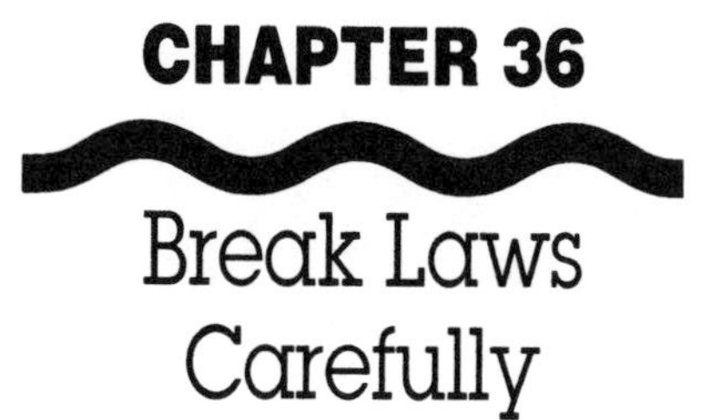

CHAPTER 36

Break Laws Carefully

In 1987, a group of Washington bureaucrats decided that all businesses could use some additional costs, so they created new hiring regulations.

One was a requirement that every employer have absolute proof of every employee's citizenship. It was quite unforgiving. An employer was subject to a hefty fine even if the employee had professionally done forgeries.

Of course, they created new forms. This paperwork could be checked at random and anybody found in violation could be fined $10,000.

It was a modest effort but it had the desired effect. It raised costs a little so businesses would have to raise prices a little, and it raised taxes so the government could hire more bureaucrats.

Life was grand except for those who actually produced something — we had to live in regulatory purgatory, where the pain went up but there was a little chance of salvation.

At Checks To-Go, a PC peripherals company, our personnel files didn't meet the requirement. The problem was that these regulations were retroactive. All documentation was required for a year into the past.

WE SENT our controller, who was also our personnel

director, to a $295 seminar explaining the new regulation. The controller was Cathy White.

At the seminar, Cathy saw several lawyers "tsk-tsking" about the unreasonableness of the new law but warning of the severe dangers of noncompliance. Cathy also heard the lawyers offer further assistance outside the seminar. She just stayed and listened. What she heard was bad enough.

To follow the law literally, we had to add an item to the personnel file that shows proof of citizenship for all twenty employees hired for the previous year, with a copy of either their birth certificate or passport.

We followed this regulation and it took about eighty hours of work, but two months later Cathy came to me with a solitary problem. One employee, Don Silver, had been hired as a customer service representative eight months earlier, but it didn't work out and he left after two weeks.

Life was grand except for those who actually produced something. We had to live in regulatory purgatory, where the pain went up but there was little chance of salvation.

When we checked our records and then back with his former employers, we couldn't find proof of citizenship anywhere. The law said we needed proof of all recent hires' citizenship or we were subject to a fine.

Cathy called one of the seminar experts.

"You should hire a private investigator. That will at least show diligent effort if the question of this employee is raised," suggested this uneconomic being.

Cathy asked me.

"Let it go, break the law, and we'll run the risk of a fine," I said. "This guy was on our payroll for two weeks many months before this law was passed. We've complied with the law concerning all the new hires, and besides, no one has ever followed up. Look, hiring an investigator to chase this down is ridiculous. What could be gained? Nothing. The only thing that changes is we spend less time working, which means we make less money and pay less taxes."

Cathy, who was a very responsible employee, reluctantly agreed.

We discussed it at length, and I explained it was always company policy to obey the law but sometimes there would be contradictions. Sometimes proper compliance merely reduces profits and raises costs so prices go up and taxes paid go down. Everybody loses.

Do-nothing regulators are the best you can hope for. Do-something regulators end up requiring OSHA-mandated backup sirens that also happen to violate many municipal noise ordinances, or demanding documentation of the racial mix on your payroll in direct contradiction to laws against recording such information.

People have been writing laws in this country for more than 200 years. Sometimes they don't match up. Sometimes, the laws or regulations simply can't be done. When that is the case, tell the next manager up and break it. When lawbreaking is necessary, the CEO must bless it, or there will be anarchy. Here's how to free your crew from ruinous rules without creating chaos:

1. Never let anybody break a law or regulation without first discussing it with his or her superior and documenting

it. The only reason to ever do this is when it is inherently impractical or contradictory to another law. That superior manager is responsible for letting his or her next level up know. In other words: Let the CEO decide. That's why CEOs make the big bucks.

2. Double your efforts to keep the spirit of that law. This is no defense, but it can't hurt and sometimes, in a rare moment of rationality, it will be recognized as absence of malice. In an area of impossible record keeping, don't display arrogance by never doing it. Create half-hearted records, but save your time for more worthwhile projects. This lets regulators save face. And should they check, you might get off with just a wrist slap.

3. If your company benefits economically by ignoring a law, you may be kidding yourself. Be triple careful. If noncompliance creates safety hazards for employees or some level of risk to your customers, don't break the law. Just don't, or your mom (and millions of others) will see you sweat on *60 Minutes*.

PART 5

SPEED: Running Under Sail

CHAPTER 37

Turn Around Your Business

In 1975, Fisher-Price realized it had an inventory problem. Shortly thereafter, Montron didn't have any money. The inventory was Montron's hand-held movie viewer, which we had sold in increasing numbers to Fisher-Price. The problem was that the inventory system missed two shipments of movie viewers that Fisher-Price had bought from Montron but then never sold to retailers.

When the surplus was found, all future orders with Montron were canceled for six months.

We had been growing rapidly up to then, getting larger and larger orders from Fisher-Price as well as pursuing other areas. Sales, mostly from movie viewers, had jumped from $100,000 to $1.1 million to $3.4 million to $6 million in four years. Fisher-Price had been buying all the movie viewers we could make for the United States and Canada. We had licensees sending us royalty checks for the viewers they made for Latin and European markets.

We also made an upgraded version of the hand-held movie viewer, the movie theater. It had its own TV-like screen and it could also project. It was declined by Fisher-Price but picked up by Sears, who sold it at $30 retail.

Our plastic injection molding division was making new medical parts for Cooper Labs and Hewlett-Packard. It was also developing its own line of throwaway medical products. And an engineer came up with a better way to measure blood pressure. He set up a separate division to develop that product, and he nurtured interest from two major medical suppliers.

There were five vice-presidents, including myself, and we hired a staffer from the Boston Consulting Group to guide our entry into the educational markets.

And finally, we were developing "The Talking Book," with a postage-stamp-sized record embossed on each page of children's books. A cigarette-pack-sized player snapped onto the record. When the child pushed the button, it played for 60 seconds and the book "talked."

All these successes and planned developments made things rosy at Montron.

But then the Fisher-Price president, Henry Coordes, called from New York and told us about the surplus. Suddenly, our major source of income vanished for the next six months. Just like that.

IT WAS QUICKLY clear that all our rapid growth had been consuming cash, and so was the development of The Talking Book, which we had agreed to market within a year. Our rights to use Disney and Sesame Street depended on that schedule.

Choices were easy. There weren't many. The medical work was spun off for much less than we could have hoped for if we had finished it ourselves. The injection molding division stopped spending so much on new development and went back to a pay-as-you-go business, developing new products only when a customer could pay for it. Three vice-presidents, the consultant, and two education-marketing employees were released. I spent more time working on anything to get immediate cash. I had no more new product work.

When we asked, Fisher-Price agreed to advance cash

to keep us in operation. We showed them everything: the impact of lost orders, the slashing of expenses it required, and how shaky the company was. They knew they could be liable if our company failed since some of the orders canceled were, arguably, binding.

As part of the agreement to advance some cash, Fisher-Price received exclusive rights to The Talking Book.

Development of The Talking Book went ahead on schedule and became the hit of the industry in a year. It was followed by other Montron developments: the Fisher-Price Tape Recorder and the Record Player, both best sellers.

Even though Montron was faced with a major crisis, quick action saved the company and ultimately made it stronger. We spun off some distractions, concentrated on our strengths and did the things that brought in immediate cash — all good stuff. Anytime.

When boats go aground, some sink but some captains know how to refloat themselves and cruise onto better things. When your business hits shallow waters, there are several things your emergency drills should include:

1. Cut costs and do whatever you must to quickly restore a pulse of cash. You can't think clearly while you are bleeding. Trim overhead and executives first. You need the sail-hoisters and rowers much more than the first mate and purser when the boat is taking on water.

2. Take a quick scan of every segment of your business and jettison anything with a poor gross margin. Everybody has to have an oar in the water now. Throw overboard anything with promises of future profitability with nothing but expenses now. There are no smooth waters tomorrow if you sink in the next five minutes.

3. Establish a new tack for this lighter boat the minute you pull out of the shoals. You are sailing faster now with this reduced weight, but you need to think about the future and develop some new products as the sails refill and the course is reset. Nothing is forever, including this recovery.

CHAPTER 38

Promote Offbeat Thinking

Probably the best outfit a graduate could hire on with in 1964 was Lennox Industries. I felt it then; I still believe it. Lennox was headquartered in Marshalltown, Iowa, about an hour of beanfields northeast of Des Moines. When I interviewed there, I stayed at the Hotel Tallcorn.

Lennox made furnaces. You bend some metal, weld it, wire it, and put some controls and a fan in it. That's all. No high tech, just solid manufacturing.

The workers at the Marshalltown factory, like those at the other two Lennox factories, did the job with less fuss than competitors in other parts of the country.

Every executive worked his or her way up. When I first started there, I spent several weeks with a dealer. I was always kneeling in spidery crawl spaces and climbing through cluttered basements. I was changing filters, lubricating pulleys, and installing sheet metal. I was dirty.

Then I did a stint on the drafting table designing ductwork and layouts. I also learned how to calculate heating and cooling requirements.

This was real stuff. There were no junk-bond plays, no strategic analysis. Lennox was grounded in reality and making money. This was American business surrounded by farms, an American Gothic company.

But that didn't mean it was slow. That year, Lennox invented the Direct Multizone System, a system that could heat sixteen rooms separately. It made flexible classrooms with movable walls possible so buildings could transform with the changing enrollments and curricula.

They also invented a heat exchanger that didn't stress the metal and therefore didn't make those familiar annoying ticking noises.

These things happened because creative thinking was pursued, almost worshipped, in an environment that never got dreamy or out of touch.

Lennox also observed the effects of spray cans about twenty-five years before anybody thought about fluorocarbons. Their technicians noticed heat exchangers in beauty shops were corroding in years instead of decades so Lennox developed a ceramic cover that protected the metal.

They were always looking for a better way to do things, while continuing to do them. This spread into marketing. Forrest Locey, the Columbus, Ohio, sales manager, discovered the industry's most economical way to sell air conditioning. Roses.

II WAS THE 1960s and every wife was a housewife, and every house in a neighborhood was occupied during the day. The marketing plan was this: Every time someone in Columbus bought a Lennox air conditioner, a florist delivered a vase to that customer on the day of installation. Then every day for the next five days the florist came and delivered another single rose.

Locey reasoned, and he was right, that by the sixth day the whole neighborhood would go crazy trying to figure it out. On that day, the florist delivered another rose in a vase to each of six adjoining homes in the neighborhood; two to each side and one in front and back. Each rose was accompanied by a simple Lennox card and a note about the pleasures of air-conditioned comfort.

Normally, a neighborhood sale followed within a week. Total cost: eleven roses that were volume priced because deliveries were scheduled all over town every day.

John Norris, the president of Lennox, praised Locey publicly for being an original thinker and told the "roses" story to audiences with pride.

TWENTY YEARS later, his son, an MIT grad and now CEO, began pursuing a dicey technology that General Electric had but wasn't developing. The technology was called "pulse combustion." It carefully controlled ignition so the expansion during combustion expels the exhaust and almost all the heat can be wrung out of it. (Every conventional furnace puts about 30 percent of the heat out the chimney and into the atmosphere as the way to carry the gases up and outside.) Waste was practically eliminated with "pulse combustion," and there was less pollution. The furnace costs more, but customers realized a payback in lower fuel bills.

Offbeat thinking gave Lennox a superior product, a commanding market position, lower fuel bills to customers, and cleaner air. In the stodgy old furnace business, yet.

Here's how to tighten your ship while loosening thinking, to sail faster and foul less water:

1. Make sure every manager does some dirty field work. Handle customer complaints. Do a service call. Don't have planners. Let those who live with the plans make the plans. Make the sales crew spend time in the lab, and get the scientists out to meet customers. Transfer people between departments to keep walls from forming.

2. Once employees understand practical things, encourage unconventional thinking. Require managers to come up with better ways. Celebrate innovation: Write about it in the company newsletter. Make half the stories about failures and be sure to applaud those experiences.

3. Enhance this grounded attitude with outside ideas.

Use your CPA firm to streamline your accounting. License ideas from others. Let the bank do your pension and payroll. Use reps instead of your own sales force. This outside contact brings in new ways.

CHAPTER 39

Watch Cash

Acucobol is a model growth company.

It was founded in 1989 in San Diego and was profitable in its second year. By 1992, its sales passed $4 million. Dr. Pamela Coker, the founder and CEO of Acucobol, says part of the secret is stated in Chapter 2 of this book: Specialize to Win. "Acucobol zigs when the market zags," she claims.

In other words, they manage the business like a business, not like an art form. Their business is software.

Acucobol-85, the company's major product, is unique because it interacts with more than 500 other software platforms. Acucobol's business is built around COBOL, the most common software language in the world, yet the least trendy. All the competitors work on products directed at the newer languages, despite the fact that COBOL dominates the primary users. That is Acucobol's differentiation — that's how they specialize.

And although there is art to what they do, how they do it is pure business.

"We make a profit every month," Coker explained one time. "And the funniest thing happens when you make a profit every month. You end up making a profit every year."

IN THE MAIN office area, there is a large chart that is

one of the most popular spots in the whole place. It's like the water cooler, only it means something. The chart, posted daily, shows cash collections for that day. It is looked at, checked, talked about, and updated daily.

Everybody at Acucobol knows the status of cash flow. They know its importance. As a result, everybody knows what is important to business, and nobody ignores cash flow.

Receivables are viewed as nothing more than test marketing until they are paid. There is no sale assumed, no customer satisfaction believed and no commission paid until the money arrives.

Collecting for those sales at Acucobol serves two function's. It gets cash in the bank and it uncovers problems quicker. Aggressive collections work, and everyone, especially sales, gets involved.

In October 1992, Coker was having trouble collecting from her German distributor. She scheduled a conference for 200 European customers in Frankfurt and had all the bills sent to the partner. Her brinkmanship included a showdown at the hotel demanding $50,000 prepayment the night before the conference began. She had arrived from America with no cash, so she couldn't pay the bills herself. Under pressure, the German managing director paid the $50,000 on the spot in order to avoid embarrassment. The story ended happily, with all the past-due bills paid before the conference ended. Future collections were easier.

Acucobol is a hot company with unique technology, great margins and fast growth. It also has an open-book policy that encourages its 90 employees worldwide to examine and learn about the numbers in monthly financial statements. If an employee doesn't understand financial statements, Acubol teaches the person how to interpret them.

Acucobol is destined for greater things because it is managed tight and cash flow is watched critically. When you set sail for the horizon, there are a thousand waves between you and that line. Each one is called cash flow, and each one can capsize you. Here's how to stay afloat:

1. Every bad debt starts out as a slow pay, so stay on top of collections. High receivables and high inventory are trouble signs, not assets. Either one can be your best early warning that your service or product is slipping while your income statement shows profits.

2. Have your payroll done outside so FICA payments are made automatically. This protects against the temptation to "borrow" from the government when cash tightens. Those who dip into the government's money end up living in the "big house."

3. Never confuse borrowing with positive cash flow. Proper accounting says it is, but that's short-term thinking. Sales revenue collected is the only true cash flow. All else is temporary.

CHAPTER 40

Demand Straight Talk

Imagine a CEO saying this to shareholders:

"In early 1988 we decided to buy 30 million shares of Fannie May. We had owned the stock some years earlier and understood the company. It was clear to us that management dealt superbly with inherited problems and had established the company as a financial powerhouse — with the best yet to come."

"After we bought about 7 million shares, the price began to climb. In frustration, I stopped buying. In an even sillier move, I sold the 7 million original shares. I wish I could give you a halfway rational explanation for my amateurish behavior. But there isn't one. What I can give you is an estimate of the profits we didn't make in 1991 because of this mistake: about $1.4 billion."

THAT MESSAGE is on page 16 of Berkshire Hathaway's 1991 annual report. Its chairman, Warren Buffett, always uses straight talk and highlights his errors. Here's the good and the bad, he seems to say. *Here's the truth.*

The truth eliminates many other negatives. When people are straight, espionage budgets and efforts drop. The propaganda budget goes way down, and so does the ammunition budget. You no longer pay for second guessers and checkers who slow everybody down, because everybody is trained to talk straight.

What goes up are profits.

Buffett also knows how to talk about profits and risk. In his 1990 report, he predicted some bad results as well as some good results from a new business venture in supercatastrophic insurance. "We are not spreading this risk, we are concentrating it," he wrote. "We expect this to produce satisfactory results over, say, a decade, and we're sure it will produce absolutely terrible results in at least an occasional year, but I have always preferred a lumpy 15 percent to a smooth 12 percent."

This kind of straight talk has produced a company culture that operates many billions of dollars in business revenues with just a few people at headquarters in Omaha, Nebraska.

At Berkshire Hathaway, if you fail to perform you are asked to explain. If you deceive, you are gone. Turnover is low. The result is reduced operating costs because the staff is smaller and more attuned to business than to reading between the lines. This boosts profits.

When commands are clear and to the point and everyone says what they mean, sailing is quicker and drier:

1. Put some bad news in your employee and customer newspaper. Tell everybody a few of the things that are not going right. Readership will jump, the good news will be believed, and an air of trust will begin.

2. Deflate pomposity and puffery in meetings. Attack it. This is a threat to everyone's survival. If it ever becomes institutionalized, you will lose the ship, cargo and crew.

3. Terminate liars. Be rather public about it. Put this in your handbook as a company policy. Deception is lethal. Bad news at least defines the problem. Lies hide problems and help them grow.

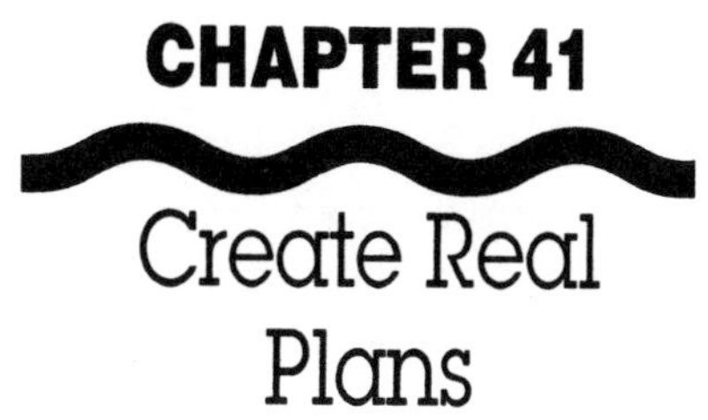

CHAPTER 41

Create Real Plans

No surprises. That was the rule in the 1960s and 1970s among the corporate staffers at Honeywell who dreamed of a world where everything went according to plan.

And so they did their absolute best to create that world. They had their large staff of "training" people organize seminars to teach everyone how to plan. This was planning to plan — one step shy of planning to plan to plan, which is the sort of thing a vice president of special projects would leap at in a big company.

A cycle was organized, and each division was to present an annual report to the corporate office. The presentation took half a day and was attended by all the top officers. The plan was given to all in three-ring binders and then read, word by nonspontaneous word, by the managers. Just another zany group of hang-loose executives.

The plan was supposed to set out everything that would happen during the year. No further meetings would be necessary until the next year. If the plan was good, it would work and no changes would be necessary. All that was necessary, we were lectured, for the plan to be effective was for the planners to think hard — herniate our brains.

OUR DIVISION imported Rollei cameras from Germany,

Pentax cameras from Japan, Elmo movie equipment from Japan, distributed Nikor darkroom equipment and manufactured some items domestically, such as a slide projector and the Honeywell Strobonar line of electronic flash units.

We started with a product plan and competitive assumptions. We knew there would be a new Pentax camera, and we assumed it would boost spring sales. We also knew two new compact flash units were coming, and we assumed those would also add sales. Just like that — product plans became sales assumptions.

It took only two months. At first, sales refused to commit unless prices were frozen and known, and production refused to give prices until sales were predicted. The balance was beautiful, if you're into that sort of thing. And it seemed we were.

The logjam finally broke when sales gave a forecast; then production relented and responded with cost estimates. Finally, there was some semblence of revenue and costs so the year came together.

Every brain herniated.

From this, departmental budgets were created, with great negotiations, as each department head pleaded for more people, equipment, and time to work on the plan.

This was planning to plan — one step shy of planning to plan to plan.

Six months later, it was done and everybody understood and even semisupported it. Our ad agency and our PR firm anxiously awaited it, so they could plan their year. This was "the word" according to Honeywell, and the Honeywell planners were happy.

Then, three days after the plan was submitted, Minolta announced a new camera at prices that were 18 percent below ours.

AN INTELLIGENT response would have been to match the price with the new Pentax, but that wasn't in the hard-thought plan. Everyone had thought really hard on it, and then our thoughts became really hard. We decided to hang tough and see what would happen.

The inevitable happened. Minolta took the number one sales position. We reacted too late to stay in the lead. Vivitar, meanwhile, continued their steady takeover of the flash market, passed by and didn't look back. We had seen their threat years before, and even planned for it. We set up a Japanese manufacturing base to compete. What a plan.

They, meanwhile, didn't set up any base but continued to shop all over the Orient for the best pricing. Their plan was better, and their operating margins were 10 percent ahead of ours as a result.

We planned again. This time we planned to sell more units in Japan, but it was too little too late. We had thought really hard about our plan. We wrote about it, talked about it, and at the time it seemed workable. In retrospect, that was the difference between us and Vivitar. They weren't talking only to each other, as we were. They were talking to customers and vendors. While we were still planning, they were living the plan and making adjustments.

Then, within six months President Nixon put in an (unplanned) price freeze, the yen made an (unplanned) devaluation, and suddenly gasoline was (unplanned) in short supply. Customers became nervous and stopped buying anything, which, of course, was unplanned.

Too many plans are written in this vacuum. They are so rigid that they are unreal and therefore unused. They become piles of paper. Here is how to chart your course in ways that handle rough seas and shifting winds:

1. Make plans quickly. Don't let the process drag on. It doesn't get any better with more time. Avoid absolute predictions of where the economy, costs, markets, and competitors will be. Use broader philosophical statements of what changes will be made if the economy dives or soars. Those judgments are smarter when made in advance than during the trauma of radical change. If plans are realistic, they can be helpful. Base the strategies on your strengths and admitted weaknesses and assume some unexpected events.

2. Put in short-term, monthly, or quarterly checkpoints to alter the plan. If revenues don't hit a certain level by May, do not assume a hockey-stick-shaped sales curve for June. Adapt to short-term results — monthly or quarterly. Markets affect you more than you affect markets.

3. Examine all the plans in your company. If they are not dog-eared after six months, stop producing them. Plans are working documents, not credenza decor. There should be enough background in the plan that it is sometimes used just as reference material. It should also be used every month as a checkpoint on progress and to guide changes when results exceed or fall below the projection.

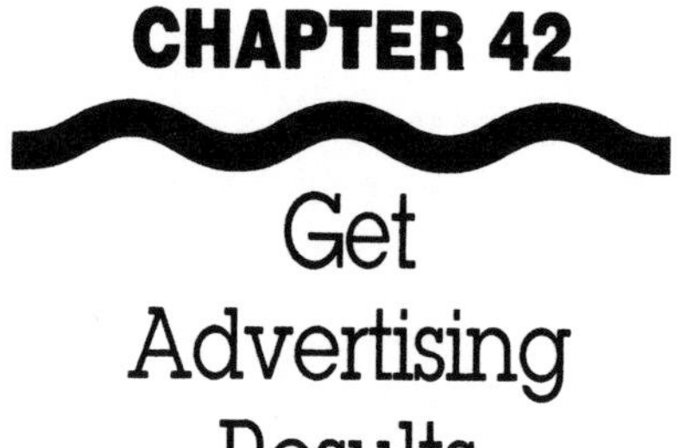

CHAPTER 42

Get Advertising Results

Honeywell Photographic had two new cameras to introduce in the fall of 1970. It was advertising manager Felix Pogliano's job to introduce both to the public.

The cameras were quite different. The Rollei 35 was the first pocket-sized 35mm camera. It was rugged. It had Zeiss lenses with a Compur shutter and a built-in light meter.

Felix knew a simple truth. Advertising efficiency can be enhanced more by simple measurements than by any other expense item in business.

So he started with the assumption that this was an outdoor camera. You've got to test advertising, but you must start with a few assumptions. Felix placed introductory ads in *Sports Illustrated, Field & Stream,* and *Skiing*. Other ads were placed in *National Geographic* and *Time,* just to compare their response rates.

The next assumption about camera advertisements was that color costs 50 percent more but generates only 20 percent more inquiries. This assumption was based on past history.

Every ad in every magazine was measured by its cost per inquiry, which ranged from $10 to $50. A word about the word "inquiry." We assumed that for every inquiry there were about another 100 people who read the entire ad but didn't respond. So the price per inquiry was really the price to reach 100 interested readers.

THE FIRST ASSUMPTION proved right. The cost per inquiry in the active-sports media was about $28. The cost per inquiry for the news magazines and *National Geographic* was about $45. The assumption was proven, and the decision was made — go with the active-sports media.

A number of ads were purchased, each using different headlines: "Big Pics; Little Camera," versus "Affordable Rollei Quality," versus "Great Action Photography from a Camera That Fits in Your Pocket," and so forth. Finally, we found ideas and words that dropped the cost down to $12 per inquiry.

Once the proper headline was found, Pogliano tested a full-page ad and quarter-page ads and reconfirmed suspicions that there was no reason to put a small camera on a big page.

After a year of testing and measuring, the ads were so effective that they were selling through retailers, with less than 4 percent of the sales going back into advertising. Every ad placed tested at least one element.

The problem was the product. It couldn't be advertised effectively, and effective advertising proved that.

Honeywell then started advertising the Rollei 35 at different saturation levels in different parts of the country. They tried heavy spring advertising in the northeast and southwest, without any spring ads in the northwest and southeast. Warranty card returns were then measured by state against the dollars spent to see how much the heavy advertising actually increased sales. Budgets were then adjusted.

Eighteen months after introduction, the advertising budget was slashed from $1 million to $150,000 per year. There was just as much product movement and $850,000 in additional profits.

Advertising, in this case, worked. And as Pogliano tightened the advertising ship, Honeywell's profits grew.

BUT THE OTHER CAMERA, the Spotmatic IIa, had a tougher time. A lot tougher. This was a conventional single-lens reflex 35mm camera, with a twist. Honeywell designed and Pentax built in a flash meter. Right into the camera. The flash meter always measured straight ahead, so the flash could be bounced off the ceiling for softer shadows or held out to the side to create more shadows across the subject, and the camera would still measure the light properly. When these effects were used, the camera compensated for reduced flash intensity.

The Spotmatic IIa had a tough time because it was hard to define. (We just used about 75 words to describe it.) The ads didn't do much better.

It was a new concept back then, and introductory ads were placed in *Popular Photography, Modern Photography,* and other "fan" magazines where the readers understood photography. Cost per inquiry in these books typically ranged around $5. Readership was heavy, and readers were interested in photography. But the best we could do was $175 per inquiry. The message wasn't getting across, and our agency, Campbell-Methun was feeling the heat.

We invited Tracy-Locke, a competitor, to take a look. Their account executive reviewed what was happening, furrowed his brow, and left. One week later, he invited us to lunch, saying he thought his creative group had "cracked the code."

We couldn't wait. At lunch, the account executive, an upbeat Texan, eagerly showed us a proposed media schedule with several changes in advertising. "We're going to set new records for you. Your cost per inquiry will plummet," he purred, and poured another Sauvignon Blanc.

We were in a reserved side room of the restaurant, and the walls were lined with charts and graphs. He proved we would end up with eight to ten times more inquiries if we inserted reply cards with every ad in the photo hobby magazines. This would work even if we ran half as many ads, he said, sure of himself. "We've done this for so many other clients."

He continued. If we expanded into consumer publications like *National Geographic, Time, Newsweek,* and the like, we could generate a larger response. The best thing to do was to put a coupon on the advertisement with the words "Free Brochure" on it in bold type.

We thanked them. We wouldn't let them pay for lunch, and we had no intention of even calling them for a few days. It was embarrassing. Not them, us. Their ideas weren't bad, but our guidance was way off. Inquiries were never the goal. Sure, they could get us inquiries, but different kinds. Inquiries were merely an indicator of an ad's broader effectiveness.

At the same time, Campbell-Mithun held several focus groups with camera users to explain the features of the Spotmatic IIa. They got better and better at phrasing it, and they continually rewrote the ads. Results finally improved from disastrous all the way to merely poor. We quit trying.

THE PRODUCT DIED within six months. As Chapter 5 says, if you can't write the headline, kill the product. We lost $500,000, as professional explainers tried to explain an inexplicable product. The problem was the product. It couldn't be advertised effectively, and effective advertising proved that.

The choice of media is the most important advertising decision. Next is what you say. The least important, oddly, is how you say it. Creativity still counts, but it's not nearly as important as where you say it and what you say.

In business, advertising is your foghorn — here's how to use it:

1. Never run an ad that is not testing something. Start with media comparisons, where differences in effectiveness typically run from 10 to 1, strongest to weakest. Next, test the basic message. Different approaches vary in response by four times or more, best to worst. Test the size or length of ads and measure saturation levels.

2. Manage the agency tightly. They maximize their profits by running expensive ads a few times. You may do better with cheaper ads run a thousand times.

3. Advertising has only one purpose: to sell more product. Image advertising is a waste; never fall into that trap. If selling more product won't help your image, why be in business? Advertising does not close the sale in most businesses, but that is no excuse for ignoring the sales objective. Stay the course.

CHAPTER 43

Cut Costs with Higher Quality

Fisher-Price has a basic philosophy. It says toys must have lasting play value. That means that they cannot break and that kids must stay interested long after the newness wears off.

Durability is tested by drop testing and by endurance runs. Lasting play value is stop-watched over a period of weeks in a private school run by Fisher-Price for local Buffalo kids. The kids choose from among 100 toys every day.

I joined the culture in 1976, when Fisher-Price bought Montron. (Chapter 37 explained this shotgun marriage.) I was marketing vice-president at Montron. After the sale, I became managing director of AFI de Mexico, our manufacturing subsidiary, and also general manager of Fisher-Price West Coast.

Fisher-Price and Montron developed a record player together. The design was difficult, and we each saw shortcomings in the other.

"You guys don't have a clue how to design a knob for kids that is easy to use and will not break," sneered Tom, Fisher-Price's head of product development for the audio-visual category.

"God help you if you ever have to design something with more than ten parts, or something that moves," I shot back. We were both right, and both myopic.

The truth was, Fisher-Price's philosophy elevated us at Montron. No matter how much smarter we thought we were, or how much Tom's taunts drove me nuts, we in fact benefited immeasurably from this philosophy of lasting play value.

Our record player cost more because of this philosophy, but it was unbreakable and couldn't scratch records nearly as easily as the competitors'.

And then there were the solder joints. I knew a thing about solder joints. When in high school I interned at the Atomic Energy Commission, soldering cables used on a synchrotron particle accelerator. Fisher-Price's standards for solder joints, I later learned, were light years ahead of the Atomic Energy Commission's.

It was standards such as this that gave Fisher-Price its reputation. When our record player came out, about two dozen cheaper models were on the market that year. In the second year of the Fisher-Price record player, all 12 other players sold together about as many as we did. Ours was by far the top-selling record player of all time.

> This is trust, and it is based on quality. It saves advertising dollars, returned products, bad feelings, and the cost of redoing the entire product line every year.

THE PHILOSOPHY OF QUALITY leads to money. When toy buyers came to the toy fair in New York City, the difference jumped out. Buyers would walk into the Mattel showroom and look at a media schedule for new products. They might commit based on that. Sometimes, they hung around to see the ad, and once in a great while they looked at the product itself.

But when buyers went to the Fisher-Price showroom, they didn't see any media schedule unless they were persistent and lucky and stumbled across somebody who knew it. There might be a few ads, and those were sometimes examined. But inevitably, what buyers were looking to see from Fisher-Price was the product. People buying Fisher-Price were buying product, not advertising.

When parents shopped, it was the same. They might seek out a G.I. Joe and its accessories, but they would never know who made it. But they would go to the Fisher-Price section and find a Fisher-Price toy they liked even though only minutes before they were unaware it even existed.

This is trust, and it is based on quality. It saves advertising dollars, returned products, bad feelings, and the cost of redoing the entire product line every year.

While we at Montron were becoming successful thanks to this guiding philosophy, another group of designers back in Buffalo were trying an improvement on another basic product — the kite.

The Fisher-Price kite was supposed to be a giant step forward, and it almost worked. All the consumer had to do was take it out of the box, slip two tubular struts into a mylar-with-fiber wing, and it was ready to fly.

The kite was shaped like a bat. It had a retractable cord built in that served as a stabilizer — weighting down the bottom. To fly it you set it on the ground, grabbed the handle, and walked away. As you walked away, the kite's retractable cord played out the 60 feet of line until it hit the end. When it hit the end, the kite flipped up off the ground and, in a brisk wind, soared straight up.

The folks at Fisher-Price spent $500,000 to turn a great idea into the bat kite. And as they stood there in the brisk wind and watched the bat kite fly high in the winds off

Lake Erie, they felt sure they had a winner.

But then they tried to fly it one day when the breezes were only semi-brisk. The kite wouldn't fly. It was too heavy. Yet this was a product that passed all the specific product quality tests. It didn't break when it was dropped. It didn't even rip if it was used as third base. It was durable, the colors didn't fade, and it was nontoxic. Heck, kids could teeth on it.

Somehow, the folks who dreamed up the bat kite missed the key ingredient to quality — functionality. It did not function as conceived. In light winds, when other kites were in the air, the bat kite didn't fly. It sat fat on the ground, fluttering like a snare drum and wobbling like a penguin. They didn't "get" it. They had allegiance to a set of rules but didn't understand the philosophy.

After three embarrassing months, and a half million painful dollars, Fisher-Price quietly pulled it off the market. The project manager on the bat kite understood the rules. The kite didn't fail the drop test, and it was nontoxic. But it didn't have the thing the rules intended to protect — lasting play value. The record player passed the same drop test and was also nontoxic. It had lifetime solder joints and it couldn't scratch records; it worked and was enjoyable under normal play conditions.

Make your business shipshape these three ways:

1. Quality needs to be pervasive because when quality improves, warranty expense drops, efficiency improves, and marketing costs go down. But quality must be more than just a statement, slogan, or rules. It must be a well-written companywide philosophy.

2. You can't inspect quality into anything. If you catch 10 percent bad, you're still shipping 1 percent faulty product because inspection itself is an imperfect process. Help your

quality department pursue causes of defects and correct them instead of just catching rejects.

3. Randomly pick one day a month when you visit and do nothing but check out quality in certain areas. Make the day different each month. Do nothing else that day; take no calls, see no outside people and attend no meetings. When you go on a quality quest, spend all day quizzing the employees and customers. Ask what is happening and how it can be done better. Soon, your co-workers will pick up on this and do more. It becomes part of the culture.

CHAPTER 44

Manage with One Piece of Paper

One sheet of paper. One. Uno. Ein. Three minus two. One, one, one.

Consider Robert Vlasic, who owned and managed an auto-leasing business, a nursing home, a real estate business and a pickle company.

"I have a rule that one, and only one, piece of paper is submitted to me weekly from each business. This type of communication is critical," he once said. His point is that there are just a few facts that count in every business. If those things are happening right, everything else falls into place.

His sheet for the pickle business shows the number of cases of pickles shipped that week, by category of pickle. It shows the dollar total, gross profit and labor expense by plant. And it includes the number of hours paid by each plant for administration and labor plus overtime. It makes comparisons by the week, and by the quarter.

The pickle business grew rapidly, and the others were steady. Rapid growth often leads to loss of control, but Vlasic refused to let it get complicated. Vlasic had a broad line with 73 items, including relishes, sauerkraut, peppers and all varieties of pickles. By 1970, Vlasic had four plants and contracts with several growers of cucumbers. Still, Robert Vlasic wouldn't let it get complicated.

In 1962, Vlasic's first year, sales were $1.7 million with

profits of $100,000. By 1971, sales had reached $27 million and profits were $1.8 million.

"Grow as fast as you want," Robert Vlasic said in 1971, "as long as we keep a 5 percent profit figure." At the time, sales were $27 million. Every plan the company made was exceeded by greater growth and profits. In 1971, the officers were projecting sales of $55 million by 1975. They hit $60 million.

BUT UNKNOWN to the sales managers, Heinz, the market leader in pickles, decided to seize the ketchup market. Heinz conquered ketchup but lost out on pickles, and suddenly Vlasic became the market leader in pickles. (You can't be all things to all people. Gain ketchup, lose pickles.)

Everybody concentrated on the few things that counted — pickles shipped, overtime, and price.

It was easy. Vlasic was simply and directly managed and never let profits slip in pursuit of sales. Both came naturally, and key among Vlasic's principles was managing the entire business from one sheet of paper. It forced focus. It eliminated distraction. And everybody concentrated on the few things that counted — pickles shipped, overtime, and price.

You can run a business with financial statements, but that's like standing on the stern and reporting to the captain about how many rocks you just missed. If you want reports from the bow, instead of the stern, try this:

1. Put the management report on one piece of paper,

dropping all detail that isn't critical. Include shipments, backorders, cancellations and payroll expense as standard items. Most accounting data is historical. Add some forward-looking data such as customer credit, returns, ad response or number of inbound calls to get some sense of the market. Put in product development expense versus benchmarks. The idea is to keep one eye on the horizon.

2. Distribute this paper broadly each week so that everybody's critical number is seen by everybody else and there are no secrets. Highlight deviations, good and bad, so that everybody quickly sees what is happening.

3. Stick with it. Don't have time for other "interesting reports" that those with idle time create to enhance their status. Manage with one report and ignore all else. Schedule a meeting once a year to decide on revisions and subtractions to the report. When you revise it, don't let it grow. Each addition must mean a subtraction somewhere else. Use big type.

PART 6

GENERAL SEAWORTHINESS: Stabilizing the Organization

CHAPTER 45

Invest Simply

When the Wall Street managers smelled the money in Forest City, Iowa, they had no choice but to go there. They were players, after all, and they had turned up quite a game piece in Forest City — Winnebago Industries.

In 1987 in Forest City, population 4,100, Winnebago Industries was thriving. Orders were strong and it looked as if a thousand motor homes a week could start rolling out of the factory by year's end. Dozens of citizens of Forest City became millionaire investors. None was richer than John K. Hanson, the 79-year-old bombastic, contrary founder of Winnebago.

Hanson, who owned half the stock in the company, loved to try to outsmart the markets. In 1985, Winnebago placed a large order for Renault chassis to go inside the newest models. When he placed the order, it looked to Hanson as if the French franc was cheap, so he contracted to buy franc futures. As he bragged later, he was dead right. The franc increased so fast in value while he received, and was billed for, the Renault chassis that he ended up with, essentially, several thousand chassis for free.

Hanson showed the *Des Moines Register & Tribune* reporter the results. The company doubled profits, to $20 million, partially because of Hanson's savvy. Winnebago stock soared, and since he owned half of it, his personal value went up by $80 million.

And the guys from Wall Street couldn't come fast enough. It didn't matter that there were only two ways to get to Forest City — through Des Moines or Minneapolis — or that both required long rent-a-car drives through flat farmland to reach it. There was money to be toyed with, and these guys were players.

Winnebago met several bright money managers and investment advisers. "Last year," said Hanson of the new direction, "we made $13 million in the stock market and $9 million in the business."

THE NEXT YEAR, Winnebago acquired some IBM mainframe leases in leveraged transactions. The casino was open as the advisers were lining up stock investments, straddles, bond plays, option trades, and all the the other things financiers invent for bored people with cash.

A funny thing happened; the house won. The bond deals were mediocre, the motor-home market softened just after the factory was geared up, and the leases on the IBM mainframes were disasters. The company made only $3 million in 1988, and the stock price took a nose dive. In 1989, more investments soured and Winnebago lost $3 million.

There is only one sure way to end up with a small fortune: Start with a large fortune.

Winnebago's major competitor, Fleetwood, didn't do any speculative investing. In 1987, they didn't do nearly as well as Winnebago did. The next year, they did quite a bit better. It was a smooth, straight investment road they followed. They didn't roll the dice; they put their extra money in CDs and treasury bills. Their returns were strong, not spectacular. The second year, their returns were still strong.

Fleetwood wasn't as distracted with fancy investments. They focused on their business and, over the years, soon saw Winnebago only in rear-view mirrors. Some of it was plain old business hustle, but much of it (according to Wall Street analysts who follow the stock) was due to watching the business and not getting fancy.

If you are not *on* Wall Street, don't visit. If you don't get information faster than outside investors, there is only one sure way to end up with a small fortune: start with a large fortune.

Stick with what you know. On a ship, remember you are a sailor, not a fortune teller. Here's how:

1. Put excess cash in CDs, T-bills, and bonds. Then neither think that you are smart when you outperform everyone, nor belittle yourself when you don't. You are smart no matter what because you've minimized the effort and reduced distractions. In the long run, you will do better.

2. When you hire outside managers, use only a few. Pick them for the lowest management fee and most secure controls, and don't let them stray from the philosophy in number 1. Make part of their compensation a bonus for slightly outperforming the market. Don't give extra pay for an extremely good performance — that's a casino incentive.

3. Never review performance daily. If you do, you speculate. Soon, you are tempted to react. Invest in simple, nonspeculative uses and wait it out.

CHAPTER 46

Negotiate Faster

In 1973 at Honeywell, we needed new products.

For one thing, it looked as if Pentax would drop us as distributor for their cameras and sell direct in North America. That's exactly what happened. For another, Vivitar was killing us in electronic flash with Oriental sourcing. Our American labor rates for our flash made us noncompetitive, and we lost that market. In addition, slide projectors as well as movie cameras and projectors, were static and dominated by Kodak.

It was time to move. "How about AGFA," somebody mused in a staff meeting. At the time, AGFA was the third-largest film company in the world — close to Fuji, while both lagged far behind Kodak.

I called AGFA.

"We've got sixty U.S. sales reps and six telemarketers," I told them. "Every photo dealer in the country hears from us at least every two weeks. Some of the bigger ones see us every day."

It was a seductive song. AGFA was struggling. They had fifteen sales reps, and dealers often went months between calls. Instead of steady deliveries, AGFA dealers tended to be in heavy supply one week and out of stock the next.

TWO WEEKS LATER, I was in New Jersey riding in a limousine with Bob Copenrath, AGFA's chairman whose nickname was "Mighty Mouth." Copenrath had a way with words.

"Mr. Sutton, we would like to give you this beautiful daughter of ours," said Copenrath, in reference to U.S. distribution of AGFA film. "But you understand that she needs a nose job." That was just his way of saying that sales were flat and they were consistently losing money in the consumer division. We were interested only in the consumer division, so we decided to look more closely at its flawed nose.

We talked about the possibility of increased sales if Honeywell distributed consumer products for AGFA. The strategy was for AGFA and Honeywell to combine sales forces using 65 of the 75 available sales people. Dealers would see their Honeywell representative even more, and AGFA sales would be steadier. It wouldn't be pushed — instead of dumping large orders, they would get more small ones. The sales rep would keep AGFA in a steadier inventory, as the last item discussed on their call. Dealers would never be overloaded and never out of stock. Our sales reps wouldn't be distracted, and we assumed sales would be better.

You are not making money while you are negotiating.

When I asked about their processing lab in Flushing, New York, I was hoping they would keep it. All we really wanted to do was distribute.

Copenrath responded as only he could. "We wouldn't sell our restaurant unless the buyer takes the kitchen with it," said Mighty Mouth.

It all made sense. AGFA was not making money with their sales level in the United States, and Honeywell needed a new product. Serious negotiations began two weeks later in Denver.

WE LAID THE GROUNDWORK before we began. Up front, we told them maximum price targets we could accept on the products. We didn't pad it. Much. They later explained exactly what they needed in sales, and I don't think they padded it. Much.

We agreed to let AGFA help us set the sales figures, but only on the understanding that if their demands became frightening we would walk away and pursue other product possibilities. We had several other possibilities. None were competitive or in film, and each would take considerable time to put together. But we had other options.

It took three meetings. That's all. The price targets turned out to be reached comfortably. The sticking point was in how many items we would carry, but that was solved within 45 minutes in our second meeting as each side gave a little under the banner of common gain. The compromises were easy because both sides stated reasonable minimum needs at the beginning.

In the third meeting, we agreed to their sales targets, which were higher than what they had done previously, because the more we heard about their current distribution woes, the more the strategy seemed to make sense.

Two months later, it was signed. AGFA reduced their marketing cost and got a small sales increase. Honeywell added $5 million in sales and made some modest money on it. And it only took 60 days to put together.

You are not making money while you are negotiating in port. Prolonged negotiations build antagonism. Always go for a favorable result fast — never try to maximize. After all, delivering the cargo is what pays. Here is how to make your dock-time haggling more productive:

1. Know exactly what your minimum expectations are at the beginning. If the other side insists on something less, politely walk away. Start negotiations by expressing your best-hoped-for result, and then justify it. Give the other side reasons to accept your premise and understand your needs.

2. Never let anybody who loves negotiating do too much of it. If done well, there's some agony and sensitivity for both sides. Anyone who loves it is probably a bully. Before agreeing to anything, set a deadline for a conclusion to the whole process and explain this is in both parties' interest. There are alternatives. If you don't have alternatives, this is not a negotiation.

3. Line up alternatives before entering a negotiation. You always negotiate better when you don't need to make a deal. The biggest mistake made is talking to only one possibility before finding the next. When you have several options, you don't become desperate. Therefore, you handle each one better.

CHAPTER 47

Flatten the Pyramid

Smiley Industries was bleeding when I was hired as chairman in 1988. Work was vanishing, or so it was rumored in all sorts of areas. One third of NATO's Apache helicopters were grounded due to the firm's inability to deliver a transmission casing to McDonnell Douglas, as told in Chapter 9. MX missile-guidance-systems housings had been profitable until the peace broke out. Damn peace.

There were other troubles. Parker Hannafin was threatening to drop Smiley as a vendor for intricately machined hydraulic valves. The complaint was that the rejects were too high.

Rohr threatened to take work away because of late deliveries. So did Lockheed. We had problems with Northrup too. We were putting out 120 quotes a month, but only winning an average of 10 percent, telling us we won only when we made our worst mistakes. (Later, we specialized, as suggested in Chapter 2; we cut the quote rate to forty a month and won half of them, doubling our profits.)

When I was brought in by the frustrated owner of Davis Industries, one of Detroit's leading metal stampers, losses were running at 30 percent of sales. There wasn't enough money to meet the next payroll. The company was about five feet off the ground and in a supersonic power dive. I didn't have time to blink or it would all vaporize, including lots of jobs, even mine.

Quickly, we kneecapped some of our creditors, offering payments over time plus cash for any new orders. They agreed the better option was to go along. Then we refinanced the McDonnell Douglas business (Chapter 9) and we had enough cash to meet three payrolls. The power dive had at least leveled off into a three-week descent that was no more optimistic, but at least we had time to breathe.

We looked at the operations. A huge rift split engineering and the factory. There were nine engineers but only two spent any regular time on the floor — and those two didn't spend any time engineering. The two floor engineers reported to one boss, who had no one else under him. The boss of the two engineers reported to his boss, who reported on up a level. Neither boss had anyone else reporting to him. An organizational chart would look like a totem pole.

We changed the operations. We hired a new engineering manager who gave the nine engineers individual responsibility for about twenty projects each.

Chaos resulted. Engineers wandered the floor, from their own products to others — offering help as a trade for some help. The responsibility caused teamwork, even though at the beginning it looked confusing — entropic energy.

Hierarchies make organizations sluggish.

But there were good signs. The big aluminum coffee urn in the engineering area went from three batches a day to one half. At the same time, the coffee vending machine by the factory floor suddenly needed to be refilled twice a week, instead of once.

Even though much of it still seemed uncontrolled, late deliveries went from 40 percent to 20 percent in three months. Rockwell put us back on a preferred vendor status. The place had gone from tragedy to mediocrity and the next challenge was to avoid celebrating that.

Once the organization was flattened, it became efficient. Davis Industries breathed a sigh of relief, accepted a multimillion-dollar acquisition offer for the business, and went back to the "cushy" business of making car parts.

Hierarchies make organizations sluggish. They isolate executives and create redundancies. Layers are filters and funnels. Get rid of layers and deal with them.

The nightwatch sees the iceberg, reports it to his officer, who probably lets the skipper know, who may tell the captain. This is too slow, and there are too many layers. Here's how to fix it:

1. Reorganize to eliminate a layer in the middle. Don't listen as everyone balks and complains about losing control. Layers create less control but the illusion of more.

2. Eliminate every management position that has four or fewer people reporting to it. That person doesn't have enough to do and therefore overmanages out of guilt. Take away unnecessary responsibility and give that person meaningful tasks.

3. Split your business. Forget the presumed efficiency of scale in large organizations. Larger means more layers, which means things are less responsive. Management becomes isolated with growth. Get rid of shared services; they become arrogant. Teamwork will return, and that beats the presumed efficiencies of size every time.

CHAPTER 48

Watch for Trouble Signs

Oak Industries made burners for gas ovens. It was blue-collar honest work, but the people running Oak Industries wanted more than the bowling alleys of Illinois to display their success. So in 1979 they picked the company up and they moved it to balmy Rancho Bernardo, California.

The official explanation for the move had to do with diversifications into cable television hardware and television stations. But there was more to it than the diversifications. You could see it in their arched Spanish building atop a California hill, in the elegant courtyard, and in the terrazo tile of the parking lot. The folks at Oak Industries wanted to show the world they were "uptown."

They hired an interior decorator who was "quite bothered" that the new IBM typewriter casings didn't quite match the earthtone decor. Five dozen casings were removed and spray-painted terra cotta, mauve, and New Mexico blue.

Oak Industries acquired television station after television station all across the United States and amortized the excess prices paid over forty years as goodwill. The expense of the move and building was capitalized over ten years. The logo was redone into a contemporary angular design from the old fussy 1950s design. Everything was lavish, even the description of the company in the annual report. Oak was "a thriving communications enterprise," it nonspecifically gloated.

For a while, the bankers bought it. They kept loaning money since this "profitable" company seemed to use it well.

Wall Street jumped in too by selling numerous bonds to less-favored clients, so Oak could pay all the bills they were running up. The Wall Street firms didn't keep any for their own accounts, since that could be a conflict of interest. Neat, eh? After all, profits *looked* great.

The investors' money had disappeared into a leather-lined black hole.

AND THEN in 1984, what goes around came around. Oak Industries reported its first loss in years. "This is extraordinary," said a guy in red suspenders in Rancho Bernardo, trying to explain the loss. But it wasn't. This was just the beginning of a collapse.

No one knew what happened until people looked, and then everyone knew. The investors' money had disappeared into a leather-lined black hole.

The chairman resigned under pressure and then the board, amazed at what it had done, hired the exact wrong choice for the exact wrong reason. He was a glamorous failure. The new chairman was Ed McNeely, who was once chairman of a Michigan company called Wickes. This guy was just like the folks who ran Oak Industries in Illinois — he moved his company from the midwest to southern California.

And then Wickes took over one of the tallest buildings

in San Diego and put his name on it. Wickes pushed through reckless acquisitions until finally it all disintegrated and the company was in one of the biggest bankruptcies in American history.

The new chairman.

And Oak shrunk and bled, reported loss after loss, until it got down to almost half the size it was as a stove burner business.

While these two companies trumpeted their San Diego arrival, there was a quieter outfit also starting in San Diego. You may remember reading about them in Chapter 4.

Watch for high salaries and low incentives, inventory growth, first-class travel, closed doors, new offices and old machinery, executive lunchrooms, and heavy trade-association involvement.

AS A REFRESHER: There is nothing fancy about the Price Club, except for the bottom line. The company headquarters are still in an industrial building, as before, and the CEO still has a bookshelf made of two concrete blocks and a board. But the 1991 bottom line was $129 million. The bottom line is the only appropriate place to flaunt wealth.

Everywhere else, you have to watch for trouble. Oak Industries didn't understand. Neither did Wickes. Both were flying high when they decided to "fix things," but they didn't understand that changing logos, redesigning offices, and moving are not cures for anything; they are merely proof of distraction. If you find yourself fixing things, stop. Take a shower; go for a walk.

Diversifying usually doesn't work either. High-powered telephone systems and computers cost plenty and never deliver a return.

There are plenty of places to find trouble before it shows up in financial statements. If you have empty parking lots at 7 P.M., you have trouble. If you have better relations with vendors and the press than with customers, something is wrong.

Watch for high salaries and low incentives, inventory growth, first-class travel, closed doors, new offices and old machinery, executive lunchrooms and heavy trade-association involvement. If there is grandiose publicity, deferred interest charges, capitalized R & D and pride in size rather than profits, there are problems.

Here's how to keep this dry rot from your hull:

1. Never respond to downturns with logo changes, acquisitions in other fields or changed accounting methods. Fix the real problems before touching cosmetics. New varnish doesn't fix dry rot.

2. Accounting says inventory, goodwill and receivables are assets. They are not. If your local grocery store will accept any of these instead of cash, then they are assets. They are ugly, dangerous noncontributors until they are turned into cash. Earnings aren't up unless goodwill, receivables and inventory are down.

3. There is no such thing as a perfect accounting period, or a perfect location, or perfect furniture. Changing these is guaranteed to do only one thing — cost money. Don't tamper with these cosmetics until you've had three years of true earnings.

CHAPTER 49

Sell Harder

In 1968, when Bob Hartley was 26 years old, he was hired to sell Learjets. He wanted to sell jets ever since he became an I.B.M. typewriter salesman three years earlier. He first approached Gates Learjet when he was 23, and he kept coming back monthly until finally he was hired by the Dallas-area manager, Phil Lovett, who was impressed with Hartley's persistence. Hartley sold himself.

Hartley joined a group of swaggering guys who lived and worked and wined and dined and took many rides high in the sky just to reach the annual sales quota of one. One plane at $1 million. It made for a gutsy year — all or nothing.

Hartley smiled and shook hands and then he went his way — to his office, and they all snickered as they went golfing or to Las Vegas, sometimes both, on the expense account, to wine and dine prospective clients. Hartley had other ideas.

He put together a flip chart showing the economies of owning a Learjet. His chart showed the kinds of companies and travel patterns that made it a sensible purchase.

The chart also had glossy, adrenaline-charged photographs of gleaming Learjets in flight and on the ground with exotic backdrops. Hartley wasn't completely rational.

He also did demonstration flights like all the other salesmen, but unlike the others he prefaced the flights with a couple of hours of qualifying conversation. The other salesman did the same talking, except that they did it on the demonstration flight. The information gathered during that initial conversation was essential: the person's opinion of Learjet, his or her travel patterns, and his or her financial status.

Hartley did even more preparation. He nurtured relationships with travel agencies and aircraft rental companies. Sometimes he was given information about what customers took the most flights. After a while, because he was there so much, he spotted prospects himself and then he ran a Dunn & Bradstreet report to learn of the financial shape of that particular company.

He followed with a letter to the CEO. He introduced himself and Gates Learjet in a carefully customized appeal to what he knew about the company. A few days later, he called requesting an appointment in a week. He was told someone would get back to him. He called again the next week. Each prospect received five calls. Ten new prospects were added each week.

He did this relentlessly — telling the story, finding the prospects.

Every time, it was the same. Nothing happened.

Shiny shoes and a quick smile don't hurt, but more calls mean more chances.

QUIET CHUCKLES greeted him at sales meetings when he told of how many presentations he was making and what he was doing to dig up new prospects. Some of the red-eyed salesmen pulled him aside and offered these one-sale-a-year words of wisdom: "You've got to drink with these guys. Golf with 'em, take them to Vegas. Use the expense account."

Phil Lovett stayed patient. He knew Hartley was working and he knew how this business was. Sales came out of nowhere, from everywhere, anywhere at anytime. Or maybe not for a while yet.

There was one thing in Hartley's favor — he kept his expenses down. But Hartley was getting frustrated. Later, he confessed, "I was starting to see a giant career mistake. I was trying to sell million-dollar jets the way we sold $300 typewriters. There was no indication it would work and plenty of belief by others that it wouldn't."

In May 1969, C. K. Stillwagon, a wildcat driller in Houston, bought a Learjet from Bob Hartley. That one sale brought Hartley a $10,000 commission. His annual salary was $14,000.

In June, Hartley sold another Learjet, and in July he did it again. He sold eleven Learjets in seven months and made more than $100,000. He also caused culture shock in the Gates Learjet sales department — where suddenly work occurred in places besides Las Vegas.

Selling is like every other career. Shiny shoes and a quick smile don't hurt, but more calls mean more chances — even Las Vegas understands that.

The captain who stops at five ports always has more cargo than the one who visits only one. Here's how to fill your boat:

1. Emphasize prospecting. Teach new salespeople how. Make prospecting a topic at your sales meetings. Have your top salespeople share their knowledge.

2. Display the number of calls each salesperson makes next to his or her sales results. Count letters and phone calls as equal to personal visits. Metro people can manage a half

dozen calls out of one elevator. Rural folks must use more mail and telephone work.

3. Have contests with small prizes to see who knows the most about his or her customers. Who signs the check? Who approves the purchase order? Are their sales up or down? Do they always get bids, and how many? Does the low bid always win? This is how to ensure that your salespeople are asking questions and not just talking.

CHAPTER 50

Raise Ethics, Raise Profits

When the governor of Baja came to cut the ribbon at the new Fisher-Price factory in Tijuana, we still didn't have telephones. The phone company couldn't solve our problem for thirty months.

We told the governor who, coincidentally, came to our ribbon cutting at the suggestion of our contractor. We didn't even think about having a ribbon cutting until the contractor suggested it.

We were more concerned that we couldn't get a phone line in that would let us coordinate truck crossings with the U.S. side. We had just built this efficient 60,000-square-foot building to accommodate the 500 new employees we'd hired in the previous two years. This factory was ready to go, but it needed to be able to communicate a lot sooner than thirty months.

We told our problems to the bureaucrats who had suggested the ribbon-cutting ceremony, and when they heard they told us we really should meet the governor. He knows how to get things done.

And so we had a ribbon-cutting ceremony, complete with mariachi's, free tortillas, and fruit. After the brief ceremony, everyone stood on the gravel street in front and looked at the building while kids played soccer with a can and dogs barked at the activity. The governor assured us that he could take care of things as he winked and roared off in his shiny pickup with oversized tires.

AT THE SAME SITE two days later, our contractor pulled me aside. "The governor's office called today and gave me the name of a consulting firm. They said you would know what to do with it."

I called the consultant.

An agent for the consulting firm came by with a prepared offer, guaranteeing a phone line within six weeks for a mere $10,000. He smiled and told me that his firm had expertise in cutting through red tape. "We'll take half now, and half when the phones are up," he said.

He held out a brochure. I took it and at his urging opened to the page that listed the board of the consulting firm. I recognized five names. Four were top officials with the phone company. The fifth was the ribbon-cutting governor.

It was clear. This was how things were done.

But something else was also clear. I worked for a company, Montron, that had been acquired a year earlier by Quaker Oats and combined with their Fisher-Price toy division. Before I took over the Mexican operation, Quaker Oats required I sign a statement regarding improper actions. The same statement required a new signature every year. It said:

"I will make no payments that are questionable, or that I have reason to believe are questionable, either by the standards of the country I am in or by the accepted standards in the U.S. If doubtful, I will not do it even if it makes business more difficult and less profitable. In gray areas, I will try to imagine how the transaction would look if described on the front page of my hometown newspaper, where my neighbors, high school teachers, and parents would read about it."

The guideline saved time and energy, since opportunities abounded for making creative payments at the border.

The strict rules actually made life easier — we didn't have to think about it. Forced ethics.

I told them I had no authority to make a $10,000 payment to this type of consulting firm. They smiled and said, "Be that way."

AND SO WE were — proud, ethical, and telephoneless. It was quite a fix for a new factory. But we didn't come to build a new factory by falling victim to fixes.

The guideline saved time and energy, since opportunities abounded for making creative payments.

We found a woman near the border who had a ham radio. Maria Concepcion Gonzales lived in a single-story wood-frame house, tarpaper roof, two cardboard windows and one glass window. It was about 300 yards from the barbed-wire fence separating the United States and Mexico, and we hired her while she was boiling field corn in a washtub out front. We paid her $75 a month to send messages two to three times a day to an operator on the other side, who would then telephone our engineering and transportation group in San Diego for $5 per message. It was clumsy, slow, and confusing, but it was legal and cheaper than $10,000.

Fortunately, profits and ethics are often compatible. Even more fortunately, sometimes they are not. If it were always easy, ethics wouldn't mean anything.

The foundation of your business must be ethical or you will not last long. Create a moral compass for your crew by doing this:

1. In clear, specific, unmistakeable language put limits on entertainment of clients. This is especially important in dealing with governments. Spell out exactly what kind of donations are permissible and what kind are not.

2. Rotate your buyers and don't allow any lunches, fishing trips, entertainment, or gifts. Never let buyers give "last looks" to any vendor when taking bids; that merely guarantees you get a meaningless first bid.

3. Pay your bills on time. Don't take prompt-pay discounts for late payments unless you say up front that this is part of the deal. If your controller has nothing better to do than add a day's float by issuing checks from distant banks, tell vendors where the checks will come from and in what time zone before they quote. Stealing pennies like this takes time and loses dollars in spirit.

CHAPTER 51

Ride the Big Wave

"Every long-distance phone company is obsolete," declared my pal, Ed Tuck. He wore a crewneck blue wool sweater and chewed vigorously at his ham and eggs and grits with cheese. That's Ed, 60, always biting off more than anybody else can.

In this case, in October 1989, it was beating the international phone companies. The world's phone companies! He talked in reasoned tones between bites of breakfast at San Diego's Montgomery Field Holiday Inn. Tuck is a crazed dreamer, so I listened.

"It costs every phone company in the world almost $2,000 to hook up a single new subscriber," he said in a preface to how he intended to start up a multibillion dollar company. In 1993, there are 140 million people worldwide who want phone service, can afford it, but can't get it. That's the market.

It was outrageous. Tuck explained that phone company hookup costs have continually risen over the years and that there is no way for the phone company to avoid even higher costs. "It's inevitable," he said.

That was the moment. Even before he explained his concept of a dense geodesic pattern of low-flying microsatellites, I could feel the magic. The aura. The possibilities stunned.

He continued talking, into the technical, and it wasn't boring or confusing as so much technical talk is to outsiders. What he said was enthralling, amazing. His dream was this: "A long-distance network that covers the world, especially remote areas, and hooks up customers at a fraction of the normal cost."

The words were like those that come from a street-corner schizophrenic with wild-eyed visions of grandeur. But Tuck was no maniac; he had a track record of innovation. This was real stuff.

I HAD MET Tuck in 1986 when he described to me his vision for a hand-held navigator. The idea was to create something like an oversized calculator that would take readings off satellites and tell users exactly, within a few feet, where they were anywhere in the world.

Well, it worked, and by the time of the Gulf War it was an indispensable military tool. And boat dealers were buying them by the truckload.

When Tuck first explained over breakfast his idea of taking on the phone companies of the world, I felt the serious tone in his voice. It was the same sense I got when Dean Peterson at Honeywell had gushed about the possibilities of photographic autofocus (see Chapter 5) twenty years earlier. Three striking similarities: proven people, carefully reasoned concepts, and outrageous business potential. When planets line up like this, you have to pay attention. I volunteered to help. Tuck welcomed my efforts.

After Tuck explained his idea, we set out together to make something happen. First, we needed money. Ed put together a simple presentation explaining the new phone company concept. We compiled a list of the 100 most likely investors imaginable and started sending along a one-page description of the project. We were asking for $1 million to finish the feasibility study, which would take a year. Then we called each potential investor. It was fishing, but fishing with a vision.

About twenty potential investors reluctantly agreed to sit down and listen for an hour. Our strategy was simple: If all twenty said no way, we would probably kill it and get on with life. But if we got just one or two to merely think about it for a moment, we would try two hundred more. These first twenty were little more than a sanity test.

When planets line up like this, you have to pay attention.

Any nibbles justified more presentations. We would rewrite and rehearse each time, all the while making it better.

In the first week, though, we were stunned. Our first three potential investors said yes. Yes! They wanted to give us money.

CALLING COMMUNICATIONS was born in May 1990. It was funded half by a Chicago trust fund and half by a Pacific Northwest phone company. We had to turn the other money down. That is a process for which I had no prior experience.

A dozen expert consultants were scouted out and then contracted to design satellites, do market studies, antennas, rockets, switching, patents, regulatory laws, and constellation design. They were paid less than they normally made, but got stock in the company, and to date it looks like a handsome payback one day.

They have made tremendous advances and, as of press time for *Tight Ships Don't Sink,* Calling Communications is a mere $6.8 billion from becoming a reality.

But I wouldn't bet against Calling. Motorola and Lockheed are trying, with a system they call "Iridium," that has 66 low-flying satellites. Anticipated investment: $3 billion. Cost per call was projected at $3 per minute and the worldwide capacity of the system is a skimpy 500,000.

When Iridium was announced, some investors called, panicky. "Should we cut our losses and run?" they asked.

No way. Calling will hoist up 840 microsatellites that, with a computerized switching system, creates a network that handles 20 million calls at once, with a cost below 50 cents per minute. No contest.

Calling has strong patents. Calling has the economics, and the Motorola/Lockheed announcement made us more credible. We received several million more in 1991 to speed up research, and more yet in 1992. The concept underwent revisions in heat disippation, antenna capacity, transmission through rain, and satellite oscillation.

Everytime we learned something new, we cranked it back into our calculations and it continued to look like solid numbers. One of the world's biggest phone companies looked at it, scratched their heads, and said, "Call us crazy but this just may work." It's still too soon for a conservative group like that to commit, but they made it clear they want to after we clear a couple more high hurdles. And if they don't, there's always their competitors.

One of the biggest aerospace manufacturers scrutinized the satellite concepts and said, "We can do it," while the folks at Motorola and Lockheed realized they had to reconfigure their constellation in 1992.

Then someone representing a new vault of money proposed giving Calling $10 million more in 1993. Some other guys in red suspenders seem to have $120 million they don't know what to do with for 1994. They're hanging around a lot, asking questions and buying lunch. So is it a winner?

It's too soon to know. But the odds are improving. In 1989, smart money would've bet 1,000 to 1 against it. By 1991, $3 million later, that looked closer to 10 to 1 against. In January 1993 it looks like a 50–50 bet, and bigger and smarter folks than we are are pushing their piles of green at us.

Calling is a Walmart sort of phone company, with its best growth potential in sparsely populated areas where it isn't practical to run phone lines. In 1989, there were 100 million people worldwide living in areas like this. As of 1993, there were 140 million. They all want and can pay for phone service. Half are on lists with an average waiting time of four years. The other half have no hope.

Word of Calling Communications has aroused the curiosity of many governments that simply want to know, "When will it be ready? When can we get it?"

Time, as in all things, will tell. Calling Communications may change the world a bit, making it a bit closer and some people a lot richer, or it may quietly die its own sad death. At least we'll find out.

The point is the art of dreaming is to dream the big dream, to swing for the fences with a Babe Ruth swagger. It's therapeutic. To try is to succeed. Nothing feels more hollow than wondering about what might have been.

Tight ships can ply risky waters when they want to because they are more seaworthy. Here's how to guide your business boat through unfamiliar water:

1. Hold back nothing once a new business seems sensible. Half-hearted effort kills the best of ideas. Spend heavy and fast if the market seems big, knowing some is waste. Getting there quicker pays for these errors.

2. Don't try to own exclusively, or control it. Bring in quickly as much smart money as you can. Solos never capture a market.

3. Keep your senses open while running the business tight. When that inner voice pushes you toward risk, listen.

Index